The 70 Year Train Ride

The 70 Year Train Ride

500,000 Miles by Rail

Frank Heppner

Published by Ornis Press
birdman@uri.edu

Other Books by the Author

Railroads of Rhode Island

Teaching the Large College Class

The Green Book of Grading

Islam and Islamic Science

Laboratory Manual in General Biology

Professor Farnsworth's Explanations in Biology

How a House Became a Home

ISBN 9781798925539

Heppner, Frank H.
The 70 Year Train Ride: 500,000 Miles by Rail/Frank Heppner/ -1st ed.

Printed in the United States of America
FIRST EDITION

Contents

Preface

In 2011, I wrote a little book called "Railroads of Rhode Island," to fill my retirement time after 41 years of teaching biology at the University of Rhode Island. It was published in 2012 and the publisher, The History Press, suggested I start a Facebook page to promote it. I was not a digital ignoramus, having learned Fortran in the 1960s, but Facebook, its procedures, etiquette, and pitfalls, was new to me. I duly set up a *Railroads of Rhode Island* page and quickly discovered that Facebook had an insatiable appetite for images. I quickly ran out of pictures of Rhode Island railroads and rail trivia, but I seemed to have acquired a Facebook following who wanted ever more railroad stuff, regardless of its origins or provenance.

I had been a celluloid packrat over a lifetime of taking train pictures, and had thousands of negatives, slides, and prints on railroad themes, most of which I hadn't looked at in decades. Unlike evanescent digital images, most of them were in pretty good shape, even after 60 years. By rooting through long-forgotten boxes at home, I rediscovered many of them and duly fed them to Facebook. Along with these images came something that was even more precious–memories. I had been fortunate enough to live through an enormously exciting period in railroad history. I actually *saw* cab-forward steam locomotives on the Southern Pacific Railroad, and "Big Boys" on the Union Pacific, but I had also ridden the TGV high speed trains in France, and the Shinkansen Bullet Trains in Japan. Along the way, I'd had some out-of-the-ordinary experiences, like riding in the cab of the *Super Chief* through Raton Pass, and the power car of the *Acela* through the East River tunnels.

At the prodding of my wife Marjorie, who in recent years has been one of my most helpful editors, I decided that before either the pictures or the memories faded for good I would try to organize both recollections and images, and share with other folks who are equally fascinated with trains. So here for your perusal is a lifetime of train riding and picture-taking.

Acknowledgments

No matter how experienced a writer you are and no matter how many times you proofread, mistakes stupid and otherwise always seem to sneak through, despite due diligence. That's why other eyes are indispensable. I have been fortunate to have had a number of folks who have read this manuscript and cheerfully pointed out my goofs. They include Dr. Jane Stitch, who before her life as Assistant Dean of the College of Business at the University of Rhode Island was an English teacher, Dr. Jeffrey Sack, whose dissertation committee I was on (and here has the opportunity for revenge), Mike Heppner, my son, who is a professional writer and gave me some much needed and appreciated suggestions, Dr. Marjorie Heppner, who before she became a clinical and forensic psychologist (and also my wife) was an undergraduate English major, and Everett Stuart, amateur railroader extraordinaire, who applied his eagle eye. To them, my humble thanks. However, any mistakes that managed to survive their scrutiny are mine alone.

I also want to acknowledge the hundreds of railfans and traveling companions, both family and friends, who have made this journey so pleasurable. There are too many to name but they will recognize themselves if by chance they encounter this book.

Most of all, I thank Marjorie for putting up with a husband who never grew out of trains.

Chapter 1

Thus it Was in the Beginning

In the year I was born, 1940, Duke Ellington's fabled saxophonist Johnny Hodges recorded the first riffs of what was to become the iconic rhythm and blues tune, "Night Train." The year following, Ellington himself first recorded "Take the A Train." These may have been theme song and omens for me.

I've been riding trains for over 70 years. Trains have taken me to 28 countries on four continents. In my 500,000 miles of rail travel, I've gone from the decadent pleasure of the ultraluxe *al-Andalus Express* in Spain, to the simple joys of the late, lamented *Panay Island Local* in the Philippines. Because the train had no brakes you had to jump on or off at intermediate stations as it didn't (couldn't) stop, and the toilet was a hole in the floor. I've been 700 feet under the ocean's surface in a train (Seikan Tunnel in Japan), 7,005 feet under the surface of the earth in a train (Simplon Tunnel in Switzerland), and got a chance to ride in the cab of an engine traveling 100 mph on the approaches to Boston. "Lucky" doesn't begin to describe it, but "passion" comes close to defining my relationship to trains, and I'm proud to say I'm a railfan.

I was born five years too late to experience the real golden age of 20th century rail travel, but I did have the advantage of growing up in the most beautiful city in the world, San Francisco, which was the starting point of several of the world's great train routes. Anyone born in San Francisco has very little to complain about. My dad was a doctor, and my mother was a nurse, although she didn't practice after she got married as was the custom of the time. Dad worked for the now defunct Southern Pacific Railroad (SP), and practiced as a radiologist at the old SP Hospital on Fell Street in San Francisco. The SP also had hospitals in Tucson and Houston for their employees. The Houston and San Francisco units were large

1

general hospitals. This speaks both to the regard the company had for its employees, but also to the fact that until fairly recently, railroading was a horrendously dangerous business for the people who worked in or around trains. Most of the patients were there because of injuries

My maternal grandparents lived in a small town in the California Sierra Nevada foothills, Auburn, located about 135 miles from San Francisco. It was on the SP's main trans-Sierra crossing, and had a rather unique railroad feature. The town was tiny (population 1,300) but it had two separate railroad stations. The reason was because the main line split at Auburn, one track running to the north of the town, the other to the south. The north track was always called the "up" track, because there was about a 1.5% uphill grade, and the south track, about a mile away, had the same grade but in the opposite direction, so it was the "down" track. My grandparents lived about a quarter mile from the down track, an easy bicycle ride for a kid.

Grandpa Frank had been a hard rock gold miner and had worked in the Sierras, Panama, and Korea, where my mother was born. I think it was from this side of the family that I picked up my adventurous nature. Dad's side was more scholarly. Both of his brothers were also doctors. Dad had a number of health problems, including bleeding ulcers, so he was classified 4-F at the outbreak of World War II. By 1943, the military was so desperate for doctors they drafted him anyway. Dad's surviving doctor brother was also in the army, and spent the war on a hospital ship in the Indian Ocean. My maternal uncle was in the Army Air Corps as a radar mechanic, and serviced B-29 bombers on Iwo Jima and Tinian. Dad was stationed at an Army hospital in Chicago from 1943-46. So, like many American boys of my generation, I grew up without any adult male influence at home when I was little-all my uncles and my father were gone. This is not unlike the situation today, except our missing dads were considered to be heros.

My first train ride occurred prenatally. I have a photo of my mother, obviously pregnant, in front of my grandparent's house in Auburn. Almost certainly she got there by train, using the family railroad pass, because a car trip of 135 miles (San Francisco-Auburn) was an all day proposition, and there were frequent trains. I must have been a passenger in the "baggage car."

I am, understandably, a little fuzzy on the details, but my non-infant lifelong association with trains began at about this time, starting when I was three. That's when I got my first toy engine, whose name was "Big Red." My mother kept him after I grew up and I later restored him and gave him to my son Mike. At the appropriate time I retrieved him from Mike, restored him again, and re-gifted him to my granddaughter Callie. Also about this time I received my first train book, *Smokey the Lively Locomotive,* by Lois Donaldson, which had been published in 1939. This must have been a hand-me-down because non-military publishing essentially came to a halt in WWII. Gasolene for automobiles was sharply rationed, and civilian rail travel was difficult to impossible during the war, but I have a photo of my dad in uniform,

Big Red at the station in San Francisco.

3

holding me in front of the Auburn train station on Nevada street around 1944. Non-military train travel was sharply limited, soldiers were given first priority, and the route between San Francisco and Auburn was one of the most heavily used on the West

First train book. My bored companion is Brittane, daughter of our downstairs neighbor. She grew up to be gorgeous, despite her disinterest in trains.

Coast. So how did my Mom and I get a priority to get to Auburn?

Here, as in a number of places in this communication, I am forced into speculation. Railroad employees then and now were issued passes for free or reduced rate train travel, and that benefit often accrued to family members. We had a family pass (with my name on it) as far back as I can remember. It may have been that the pass enabled my mother to pull a higher travel priority, but in any case, I'm certain that my first train ride after I was born was on the SP between San Francisco and Auburn. The first actual family train-related picture I have was taken at Auburn in 1943. It was an 8mm movie taken by my Dad of an SP cab-forward steam locomotive (more about this later) racing west on the down track.

My first *memory* of riding a train is sharp and specific. I think it was when I was about 10, around 1950. I believe my dad was going to some kind of medical convention in Salt Lake City, and he brought my mother and me. Naturally, we took the train and at that time, most American railroads had first- and second-class trains, much as Amtrak has *Regional* and *Acela* trains today. The first-class trains were the deluxe streamliners like the *Empire Builder*, *Super Chief*, and *City of San Francisco*. The second-class trains were the perfectly adequate, but slower and older brothers and sisters of the streamliners, like the *Overland Limited* (which had been downgraded after the war), the *Western Star* of the Great Northern, or the *Mainstreeter* of the Northern Pacific. Employees had to ride the secondary trains. The trip from San Francisco to Salt Lake involved an overnight run. We had

Dad goes off to war.

what was called an "open section" on a sleeping car. This consisted of a pair of facing bench seats much like on an old European train, with a wall between each of the pairs. The seats could be converted at night into bunk beds, with a curtain that could be drawn between the bunks and the aisle, giving a measure of privacy. Technically, strangers could be assigned to the upper and lower berths, giving rise to endless '40s-'60s movie comedies that were about the high jinks that were thus possible ("Some Like It Hot," with Jack Lemmon, Marilyn Monroe, and Tony Curtis immediately comes to mind).

I slept in the upper bunk. The top of the window was just high enough for me to see out as I was lying down. The sheets on the Pullmans, as the sleeping cars were known, were crisp and fresh. The car may have been

5

air conditioned, but there was a little vent by my head I could turn to allow fresh air in. It also let in the outside sounds and smells. It was a moonlit night on the Nevada desert. I could see in the distance the shadowy outline of the Great Basin mountain ranges, and there was a hint of sage smell through the vent. In 1950, the secondary passenger trains over the Sierras were usually pulled by the legendary and gigantic cab-forward steam locomotives, and every now and then you could hear the long drawn-out sound of the whistle, as the locomotive sounded an alarum for a lonely desert road crossing. The

Great-grandpa Ford.

motion of the car was gentle, and eventually I drifted off with a ten-year-old's thoughts of someday being the mighty figure who commanded the power and majesty of this wilderness-crossing galleon.

Grandpa Frank.

My interest in railroads was aided and abetted by the fact that my family had a long-time interest in documenting themselves and their activities through the medium of photography. I have a photograph of my maternal great-grandfather, taken around 1875. In the same scrapbook is another wonderful photo of my maternal grandfather, Frank Chase, circa 1905, holding the pet ocelot he

6

brought back to Auburn from his stint in the gold mines of Panama and Columbia. My grandmother, Azalea Chase, always had a Brownie 620 box camera around, and every family event and birthday was duly recorded. She would let me use it sometimes, and I loved the positive "snick" it made when the shutter button was pushed. My mother also had a Brownie.

By the time I was 10 or so, I was becoming a fairly seasoned train traveler. There were the trips from San Francisco to Auburn to see the grandparents, but one of my uncles lived in Los Angeles, and twice a year the brothers would swap visits. My uncle was an early adopter of air travel, and he always flew from L.A. to San Francisco, but six months later, Mom, Dad and I would take the train to L.A. The "streamliners" between these points were the *Coast Daylight*, and the *San Joaquin Daylight*. To anyone but a railfan, the equipment on the two was almost identical, but the *Coast* traveled south from San Francisco to Watsonville, then cut over to the coast and ran by the ocean for

The gene "railfan" is linked to another called "nerd." Fortunately for me, nerds were not picked on in the '40s as they are today.

over a hundred miles. It then went through some rather spectacular hill country before dropping down into the Los Angeles basin. The *San Joaquin* headed roughly southeast to the dead flat, and (let's be honest) boring Central Valley, then over the Tehachapi mountains, then to L.A. The *Coast* was faster, and was deemed to be a first-class train. That meant

E units at Third and Townsend station in San Francisco. Probably the first train picture I took myself. Taken around 1954.

that on our pass we had to take the *San Joaquin*. This created both a sense of social injustice, and a burning desire to somehow take the *Coast,* an urge that I was not to satisfy for many years.

One started a *San Joaquin* trip by taking a ferry from San Francisco to Oakland. On the other hand, the *Coast* route started at the now-defunct Third and Townsend station in San Francisco proper. So on the face of it, I wouldn't have had much reason to visit Third and Townsend, but the first train pictures that I'm quite sure I took myself appear to have been made at the San Francisco station. They were shot about 1954. One possible reason I might have been there was that there was a fierce local football rivalry between Berkeley (Cal) and Stanford. They swapped stadia every other year, so when the game was at Palo Alto, the SP ran special trains for football fans, like my dad, who was a Cal graduate as I later was. Were I at the station for one of these excursions I might have borrowed my mother's camera for the occasion.

My mother had chronic health problems which sometimes required months-long hospitalizations. When this happened, I lived with my grandparents in Auburn. One such sojourn was between 1952-54. It was about at this time I got my first camera, a Kodak Pony 828. It was quite sophisticated for the time, and used a roll-film variant of 35 mm film, with 8 exposures to the roll. There was nothing automatic about it, so one way or another if you wanted pictures you had to learn the rudiments of photography. For a kid interested in trains, Auburn in the early '50s was about as close to paradise on earth as you could get. You had the streamliners, you had the exotic steam-powered "fire trains" that were stationed near Donner Pass for fighting snowshed fires, but were sent to Roseville *via* Auburn for service, but most of all you had the "cab-forwards."

The cab-forwards were enormous steam engines, 121 feet long, weighing a million pounds. They were turned bass-ackwards compared to a regular locomotive, and the engineer and fireman, godlike figures, sat high above the rails at the very front of the engine. They had a distinctive syncopated chuffing sound unmistakable with any other locomotive.

During the fall fruit harvest season, entire trainloads of ice-cooled perishables cars were made up at Roseville, about 15 miles southwest of Auburn. They were called "fruit blocks." These trains were very heavy, but had to move fast before the ice melted (shades of John Steinbeck's *East of Eden*). To get them over "The Hill," as SP referred to the 7,056 ft Donner Pass, the railroad used four of the gigantic cab-forwards; two at the front, one in the middle, and one about ten cars before the end of the train. That was four million pounds of locomotive riding on 64 driving wheels. Once this assemblage started up grade it made an overpowering noise. If a fruit block approached Auburn on the up track it could be heard

5 miles away. If this train should come into town in the afternoon after school, small boys all over Auburn would grab their bikes and go to their favorite viewing spots. Mine was about a mile away from my grandmother's house, where the curving track passed through a deep cut in the earth. I'd park my bike on top of the cut so I could look down on the tracks, about 75 feet below. You couldn't see the train until it was in the cut, but you could see the towering pillars of smoke about a mile away. The sound would get louder and louder, a cacophony of pounding pistons, steam blowing off, and clacking air pumps. When the sound reached an almost painful level the ground would begin to thrum, and suddenly the first locomotive would appear in the cut enveloped in steam. You could FEEL the effort this dinosaur-machine was making.

I don't know how many times I'd seen this phenomenon, but I was dumbstruck every time I experienced it. Sitting in the cab of the first engine sat the lead engineer and fireman, magisterial in their command. The engineer always looked totally at ease, right arm casually draped on the armrest. There was a ritual involving small boys and engineers. I waved at the engineer first. I don't know if it was a union rule or something but the engineer would always wave back. Not a casual wave, but the wave of a king, from side to side. If the engineer was in a good mood he'd give the kid a reward more precious than diamonds. He'd give him a blast on the engine's whistle. The SP's whistles sounded more like an ocean liner's horn than a typical train whistle. In the cut, the sound would bounce off the walls, and would linger even after the engine had passed. That was about as good as life got for a trainstruck little boy.

There were lesser train pleasures in Auburn. There was a small freight yard near my grandmother's place that serviced the lumberyard and the feed and grain store. A small locomotive and a caboose would come up from Roseville a couple of times a week to deliver and set out a few freight cars. These little trains were called "peddler freights." If one came to town after school, I'd wander over, now armed with my trusty Pony 828. One day, I was coming home after an afternoon Boy Scout meeting wearing my uniform. I was walking along the track as was my custom, when I heard the little peddler coming down the track on its way to Roseville. I stepped aside a prudent distance and gave the engineer the statutory wave. The train passed, then to my amazement, the engine stopped. The engineer leaned out the window, and called out, "Hey, kid! Ya wanna ride?"

Einstein was wrong. A physical body *can* move faster than the speed of light if it has the proper motivation. I raced down the track, and the engineer gave me a hand up the ladder. When I was in, he said, "You can stay as long as you want, but I'm not coming back, so you'll have to let me know where you want off, and you'll have to find your way home. We

One of the Consolidations at Auburn.

The "Press Grip" with a Speed Graphic camera.

don't have any extra seats, so why don't you sit here?" The throne of Zeus. The engineer's seat.

He actually let me drive the train, dinky and clattery as it was. I wanted to stay with him til Roseville, but even I had some sense of prudence, and rode for about 5 miles. Needless to say, I caught hell because I was so late getting home, but it was worth it. I became a lifelong railfan after this experience. It is unfathomable that such a thing would happen today due to legal concerns. Too bad. I have a picture of that very engine, #2467, taken with my trusty Pony 828.

I returned to San Francisco for high school. My train activity didn't change much but the railroad industry was in a state of ferment. Diesel locomotives were sounding the death knell for steam, and after a brief burst of enthusiasm in the late '40s and early '50s, there were ominous signs that the industry was becoming disenchanted with passenger trains. In the meantime, I was beginning to enjoy catching the images of trains as well as simply watching them. My high school offered a photography course, and I was quick to take advantage of it. However, I *really* learned photography at age 15 when my father got me a summer job with a friend of his named George Shimmon, a commercial photographer. George was a dead ringer for the New York crime photographer Weegee, complete with dead cigar, and fedora with press pass. George did society, weddings, commercial, portraits; anything where the silver in film could be turned into gold. My nominal job was Darkroom Assistant. There were two "grownups" who were darkroom technicians, and my job was to do anything they didn't feel like doing. Their names were Dwaine and George (another George). Dwaine fancied himself to be an "artistic" photographer, and did all the photo studio's architectural work with the big 4" x 5" view cameras. George looked like Bud Abbott and viewed himself as a stud. On Mondays, he would always ask me if I'd gotten my "ashes hauled" over the weekend. I had no idea what he was talking about but figured he knew I liked steam locomotives. All three of them were as nice to me as could be, and I learned a tremendous amount of practical photography. For example, there is a picture of me holding a Speed Graphic, the standard press camera of the day. In it, you could see a somewhat unusual position for my left hand; it is not sticking through the hand grip. This was known as the "Press Grip." The Speed Graphics were heavy, and the platform that held the lens had sharp corners. If you were in a crowd and needed to push your way to the front, by using the Press Grip you could jab the people in front of you, persuading them to step aside (or club you, depending on how intimidating you otherwise looked). George had a contract to take some pictures at the Republican National Convention at the Cow Palace in 1956, and he let me use a Speed Graphic to get backup shots. By judicious use of the Press Grip I got close enough to the stage to get a picture of President Eisenhower.

I made a horrendous blunder in my first few weeks that almost ended my photographic career. After printing up a bunch of pictures in the darkroom, you would make sure, absolutely sure, that the 500 sheet box of expensive unexposed photo paper you were working with was closed, call out "Safe?" to be sure that nobody else had undeveloped paper out, then turn on the lights to look at your print. As usual, I was doing a series of rush jobs, and needed to see if I had gotten the exposure on the prints right. I called out, "Safe?" and hearing no response, turned on the lights. And stared into my own open box that still had about 300 sheets of now-ruined paper. George didn't fire me on the spot, which I suppose I deserved, but let me deduct the price of a new box of photo paper from my wages. I remember it was about 4 days' pay. George quickly forgot about

13

my transgression and I started going out with him as a shoot assistant for weddings. Wedding photographers have always had to carry around a lot of equipment, but in those days you could always identify an assistant photographer by the grooves in his shoulders. We had to carry two bags of equipment each weighing about 40 pounds.

It was about this point that I began my lifelong love/lust affair with cameras. George's standard camera was a big 4" x 5" Linhof that is still made in Germany (but a bit more expensive than in the day-about $10,000). There was no way I could afford something like that, but I was rapidly outgrowing My Little Pony. With my surviving wages at the end of summer I bought a used pre-World War II Exakta VX 35 millimeter camera. It was the pre-eminent camera for scientific and technical photography, and was also well adapted for railroad photography.

Cash in my pocket.

I immediately started a little business. I was not, ah, particularly athletically inclined. However, the athletic program at my high school was at the moment without a photographer, so I volunteered to take sports pictures for the student newspaper and yearbook. I quickly discovered that the athletes loved to give their girlfriends 8" x 10" glossy prints of their exploits, which I was happy to provide for a modest fee. As I used the school's camera and darkroom for this enterprise, this was a profitable business, and I was able to add extra lenses for my Exakta. One of them I still cry about. It was a 75mm Zeiss f1.5 lens that I bought for about 50 bucks. Much later, when I moved away from the Exakta system, I gave the lens away. I recently saw one like that sold on eBay for $1,600.

Caboose at Auburn.

My railroad photography improved dramatically. Like most city teenagers in the '50s, I didn't have a car, but San Francisco's public transportation system was so good that with a little shanks' mare you could get to wonderful locations for train photography. When I visited Auburn, I now looked at the trains with a photographer's eye, as well as a rail enthusiast's perspective. I was also beginning to expand my railroad geographic horizons. With the family railroad pass, I could travel anywhere at no cost. This would be almost inconceivable for a teenager today, but when I was 16, one of my "games" was to go down to the SP station as soon as school let out on Friday and go as far as I could by myself and still make it back in time for school on Monday. One glorious weekend I made it as far as El Paso, Texas, but truth compels me to reveal that I really didn't make it back exactly by Monday morning on that trip and had to serve detention, like in "The Breakfast Club." I savored every minute.

One of the distressing things about being a high school railfan in the

Coast Daylight departing San Francisco bound for San Jose.

fifties was that you got a lot of chances to make the "last run" of many passenger services. The last run of electric Sacramento Northern passenger trains between Walnut Creek and Concord was on the 13th of January, 1957 and I was on board. I was on the last SP ferry to cross San Francisco Bay on the 29th of July, 1958. I was one of the 500 rowdy railfans on the last Key System electric train to cross the San Francisco Oakland Bay Bridge on the 30th of April, 1958.

As a certifiable nerd, I also engaged in other non-railroad activities that might be, uh, questionable today. My friends and I were involved in amateur rocketry, and would whip up fifty pounds or so of reasonably explosive rocket fuel in my parents' basement to power our stainless steel rockets. We also were into "urban exploration" 40 years before the term came into general use. Around 1 o'clock in the morning on weekends, I'd sometimes sneak out of my house and join my friends for a bit of exploring of San Francisco's streetcar tunnels. At the time, there was no real subway system as represented by BART today, but there were two long tunnels, the Sunset and Twin Peaks, that were used by streetcars. Twin Peaks was by far the more interesting because it had a false roof, essentially creating a tunnel above a tunnel. The upper one was used as an inspection tunnel to give access to the overhead trolley wire for maintenance. With sufficient persistence (otherwise known as adolescent stupidity) you could travel the entire 2.3 mile length from the east portal, essentially on hands and knees, and arrive at the Forest Hill Station, where Clint Eastwood caught a "K" car in "Dirty Harry."

Our idea was to be at the opening of the Forest Hills end of the inspection tunnel around 2:15 AM which was when the bars closed and the drunks started coming down on the platform. We were invisible from the platform at that point, and could make woo-woo ghost noises. The attraction of this escapes me now but it was apparently great fun at the time. We never got caught.

Senior year came and went, and it was time to prepare for college. I got into Berkeley, but I didn't WANT to go to Berkeley (silly me). I wanted to go as far away from home as possible, and I wanted to go there by train. I was admitted to Carnegie Tech, and Rensselaer Polytechnic (RPI) in Troy, New York. Troy was further than Pittsburgh so that's where I went.

Not long ago, I found my father's worksheet for my expenses at RPI in 1958. It was $2,400 for *everything*. Tuition, books, travel, room and board, and even a little walking-around money. According to the consumer price index, that sum today should be around $19,000. Wrong. Tuition and fees at RPI are $54,000 a year now. No wonder the middle class is disappearing.

One of my favorite activities when I later worked as a professor at the University of Rhode Island was to be on hand to answer new students and parents' questions on move-in weekend in September. Over the years, there were fewer and fewer students arriving on campus by themselves, and the *stuff* they brought with them seemed to multiply logarithmically, often requiring parents to rent a trailer. In 1958, when you went away to college, that was it; you were a grownup and essentially on your own.

When I left the Bay Area for RPI, all of my worldly possessions could be fitted into two medium suitcases. I recently found the 8mm movie I took when I traveled across country for the first time, from San Francisco to Troy. It shows SP #27, the *Overland Limited*, coming in to Oakland, a shot from the vestibule of my parents and a couple of friends who had come to see me off, and the rest are out-the-window shots of the Sierra crossing. In Laramie, Wyoming things started to get exciting. I got off the train, and got pictures of a rare Union Pacific *Veranda* gas turbine locomotive, and the Holy of Holies, a UP *Big Boy*, the world's largest (subject to some dispute) locomotive– *under steam*! In Chicago, I changed over to the New York Central for the last leg into Troy. There was only the occasional trip down to the Big Apple during that first semester usually by hitchhike transport and I went home for Christmas by the same route. My mood on this return trip was a bit different; I had gone out expecting to conquer the world; I came back having come as mathematically close to flunking out as it was possible to do without actually doing so. The usual suspects played a role. I went back to New York and RPI after Christmas, but when I came west (for the last time) in June, I went back via the Southern Railroad to New Orleans, then the SP Sunset Route to LA, and then home.

My gradepoint after a year at RPI was 1.8. It was that low for a variety of reasons. One was culture shock. The coasts were vastly different in those days, and in San Francisco, I had never seen snow. More importantly, I had been #3 in my high school graduating class, but that put me about in the bottom third at RPI. Add that to immaturity and stupidity (I was 17 when I went out) and 19 credits a semester and the result was a one way ticket back home. I needed a 2.0 to transfer to Berkeley. That meant I needed "A's" in two summer courses after the second semester. Crunch time. Athena, the goddess of wisdom, was smiling at me at summer school, delivered two fat, juicy "A's" into my hands, and I became a Berkeley student, as had been my father before me. He was class of '26 and I became class of '62.

The *Del Monte* (Express or Limited).

19

For the next several years, my railroading activity took a steep drop. I started dating my biology lab partner who lived in Monterey, so I got in quite a few summer and holiday *Del Monte (Express)* trips. The *Del Monte* was a delightful little train whose cars were attached to a commuter train from San Francisco to San Jose, then its three cars were cut off, and a GP-9 locomotive pulled them through Castroville, then down to the Monterey Peninsula. It was the longest lived SP named passenger train. In its day, the *Del Monte* was heavily patronized by the elite but when I started riding it in the early '60s, it was down to a heavyweight coach, a nondescript lightweight coach, and a rather nice parlor-lounge that still had bar service, and the typical passenger, including myself, was decidedly low rent. While I was attempting to redeem my academic credibility at Berkeley, my non-study attention turned to something that was in every California boy's blood; cars. I didn't get a car, or even a driver's licence until I was a college sophomore, but I caught up with a vengeance.

If a kid wanted a car in the '50s or ' 60s, he (rarely a she) pretty much had to be a mechanic, because kids simply didn't have the kind of money they do today. My first car was an engineless '53 Studebaker hardtop–maybe a hundred

bucks. Sadly, it only survived for about six months after I dropped in a '57 Corvette engine I rebuilt from a junkyard discovery. The Studevette's replacement was another vehicle that needed love-a lot of love-to keep running; a '53 MG-TD. I quickly forgot about practicality when I saw it. A

The Studevette. Nothing from the outside would tell you there were 300+ horses under the hood.

car that had no heater, no side windows, and manually operated

20

windshield wipers was perhaps not the best choice for the San Francisco-Berkeley run, but it was so CUTE!

Providentially, it was one of the last cars made that included a crank for emergency starting. This was not quaint decor. My most memorable complete stallout was on the uphill part of the cantilever section of the San Francisco Oakland Bay Bridge sometime around 2:30 in the morning. The restart procedure was known to all MG-TD owners. 1) Put on emergency brake, 2) Extract nail file from glove compartment, 3) File corroded points on Lucas fuel pump on back of driver's seat, 4) Extract crank, 5) Pray, 6) Give it a couple of pulls, 7) If it catches, jump over driver's side door into seat, toss crank onto passenger's side, and give it JUST ENOUGH gas to get going, The MG lasted quite a while, enough to get me through Berkeley and an MS in Biology at San Francisco State University. The next step was grad school at the University of California, Davis, and it was there that my train life started up again. Before Davis, however, there was a memorable interlude.

Chapter 2

Les Trains de l'Europe:
Premier Voyage

M y first trip to Europe was in 1964, between enrollments at San Francisco State University and the University of California, Davis. As I think back on it, the times, they were VERY different. The printed guidebook student tourists used was Arthur Frommer's "Europe on $5 a Day." Yes, $5. You really could travel on that modest sum, but if you could blow $10 a day, you could be much more comfortable. "Comfortable" in this case meant that you didn't have to walk down the hall to the bathroom, or make reservations to take a bath.

You could fly to Europe, but jet service had been introduced only in 1958, and flying was basically for rich folks. Inexpensive flights to Europe didn't start until the late '70s. Most people went to Europe by ship, and the vast majority of these ships departed from New York City.

The trip from the west coast to New York City was my fifth transcontinental run. No longer on my father's SP pass, I took the *California Zephyr* from Oakland to Chicago. The one way coach fare for the whole trip, San Francisco to New York was about $130. This was actually a little more expensive than today's fares, when adjusted for inflation. The *Zephyr* was operated by the Western Pacific Railroad from Oakland to Ogden, the Denver & Rio Grande to Denver, and then the Chicago, Burlington & Quincy to Chicago (have you ever noticed that some railroad names are more euphonious than others? The ATCHison, ToPEka, and the SANTA FE is wonderful. Why, I suppose you could even write a song about it! The Winona, Mankato & New Ulm Railroad offers fewer possibilities).

The *Zephyr* comes to Oakland.

The *Zephyr* was an outstanding train from its inception in 1949 to its eventual downgrading by Amtrak starting in 1970. It was not the first train to use dome cars for scenic viewing, but as a recognition of the changed role of long distance trains in American transportation, it was the first to have its schedule specifically tailored for daytime sightseeing. When I took it, it was still using its original equipment and was very well maintained. In contrast to the Amtrak Superliner coaches used today on the same route, which have 64 seats on a single level, the original *Zephyr* coaches had 48 seats, so sleeping in a coach seat overnight was a very reasonable proposition and there were about 4 feet between seats. This might be contrasted with my most recent trip to Europe on Lufthansa (Let me spell that for you; L-U-F-T-H-A-N-S-A) where the distance between seats was a princely 31 inches. The Western Pacific and Rio Grande route through the Feather River and Colorado River canyons was one of the world's greatest train runs.

Well, all right, there was a *tiny* little glitch along the way. Somewhere in the Midwest in the middle of the night, the train jumped the tracks. A violent thunderstorm had washed out the supports for a little bridge

Putting the *California Zephyr* back on the tracks.

crossing a gully, and the rails sagged down about 2 feet. In retrospect, the engineer did a smart thing. Instead of jamming the brakes on, which might have buckled the train, he just shut off the throttle, and the train coasted over the gap. The coach I was in went "bumpity, bumpity, bump," and then came to a stop. No screaming, nothing dramatic. The conductor went through the train, checking to see if anyone was hurt, but fortunately, the only casualty was a cook in the diner who got bopped on the head with a frying pan as he was doing breakfast prep. It took about 15 hours to get us going again, because the train was in the middle of *nowhere,* but other than frayed nerves, no harm done. In my 500,000 miles of train travel, that's the only time I've been on a train that had an accident of any sort. On the other hand, I've been on three trains that hit cars at road crossings, all with fatal results. And here, I'll give you a travel tip. If you are ever on a train that hits a car, never, *ever* look out the window when the train comes to a stop. I was on the *San Joaquin Daylight,* traveling 79 mph in the Central Valley of California, when we hit a station wagon with 5 teenagers in it. The driver had driven around the closed gate. When the train stopped, the accident site was right outside my window. I never did really recover from the sight of that scene of carnage.

There was a pretty standard method and route of travel to and within Europe for poor students. You went over in "tourist class" on one of the many ocean liners that were still operating, and then got a Eurailpass. Tourist class had been renamed from "3rd class" and before that it had

24

been "steerage." I suppose this was an effort to make it sound more upscale. For my first trip, "steerage" was actually a pretty good description. I took the SS *United States*, which was and remains the fastest ocean liner ever built. Speed, rather than luxury, was the premium. For my rock-bottom fare, the cabin was located deep in the bowels of the ship on "D" deck (there were six decks above). The cabin was located at the waterline, and you could feel, rather than hear the beat of the four enormous screws (propellers). Ka-thrum. Ka-thrum. Ka-thrum. All night. Price of speed, I guess.

SS *United States* departing New York Harbor in 1964.

Kids overuse the word "awesome" today, but the *United States* truly fit the word. She was built after WWII and was designed to be rapidly converted into a troop carrier like the *Queen Mary*, in event of another European war. There were two main priorities in her design; speed (to outrun battleships) and safety (in case she got hit). She excelled in both categories. Her 240,000 horsepower could propel her 990 foot length to over 40 mph. For fire safety the only wood on board was in the butcher's blocks, the lignum vitae propeller shaft bearings, and sort of halfway in between, her one-off Steinway piano was made of a rare, fire-resistant mahogany.

The cabins in Tourist were pretty sparse, but the food in the dining room was very much like Business Class air today, on a good airline like Singapore or Emirates. Since there were two classes above Tourist, I can only imagine what the chow was like in First–caviar from sturgeon raised in bathtubs on Park Avenue. Steaks only from rare or endangered species. Breast meat from parrots who spoke six languages. (Since the writing of the paragraph above I found the menu for the Captain's dinner on the return part of this voyage in Tourist Class, June 20, 1964. "Hmm, yes, I believe I'll start with the Pâtè de Foie Gras on Melba Toast. Then, decisions, decisions. Green turtle or morel soup? Definitely morel. For the fish, the Gaspe Salmon would be nice, then maybe the Rock Cornish Game hens. Or maybe the Sirloin steak. A simple salad, then a fruit course, a pastry course, a cheese course, and a sweet fruit course. Port compliments of the Captain." Just like economy air today). The main thing I remember about the *United States* was that she was so breathtakingly *fast*. Standing out on the foredeck was like being in a hurricane.

Upon arrival in port, a traveler began taking trains. I had a 3-month Eurailpass, which is about $2,200 today for first class, but my recollection was that it was about $100 a month then. You could save a bundle by scheduling a lot of overnight trips, and sleeping on the train instead of a hotel. American train coach seats were much more comfortable than European ones, but when you're 24, who cares?

Nowadays, there is much more European travel by Americans than there was 50 years ago, and you need reservations for everything. Then, it was set up very differently, and you could be spontaneous. Every mid-and large size city had a hotel bureau in the train station. They would list only budget hotels that were within walking distance of the station or a subway stop. Almost never would you get stuck in town without a hotel, and at most you would have to *schlep* your bags for a couple of blocks.

As I remember the route of this almost-50-years-ago trip, it was: England-France-Belgium-Netherlands-Germany-Denmark-Sweden-back down to Germany-Austria-Yugoslavia-Greece-Italy-Switzerland-France, and back home. In about 2 ½ months. This was the era when the 18-day, all expenses paid, guided European tour for loud, naive Americans from Omaha was becoming the vogue. There was even a 1969 movie made called "If It's Tuesday, This Must be Belgium."

Intercity international travel was mostly handled by trains that remained more or less intact in their consist but changed crews (and engines) at the borders. The passenger cars were longer than American ones, very comfortable, but not nearly as strong as American ones and had a tendency to collapse like accordions when they hit something, which fortunately wasn't often. Each of the cars typically had a final destination, so, for example, when you boarded a long train in Paris, one car would eventually go to Brussels, another to Copenhagen, another to Cologne, etc. A removable sign on the side of the car indicated its destination, but if you didn't KNOW that you were supposed to look at the sign on the car you might have a trip rather different than the one you planned.

There was an alternate to conventional train travel that had been established in the late '50s. These trains were called TEE's, short for *Trans Europ Express*. They were all first class, diesel powered, and mostly semi-permanently coupled trainsets, rather than separate cars. They were fast, but mostly because they were limited-stop trains. My Eurailpass let me ride on the TEE's, and they provided a welcome relief from the comfortable, but

The *Settebello*.

very basic trains that were the order of the day for regular train travel. The TEE's had wonderful, romantic names. *Ambrosiano* (Milan-Rome), *L'Ile de France* (Paris-Amsterdam), *Aurora* (Rome-Reggio di Calabria). One of the TEE's was electric, and operated within Italy. It was called the *Settebello* (seven-times beautiful). That's a wonderful name for your girlfriend, but unfortunately, the '60s *Settebello* was ugly as sin. It should have been named *Verucca de la testa*, or "warty head." The engineer rode directly in the front of the train, and there was a sort of pod above him where lucky passengers could sit and get the engineer's view. A bit like the old New Haven Turbo Train, which will be discussed later. Unlike the Turbo Train however, which had an odd suspension and gave a ride much like you would experience in a quartering Force 12 wind in a *Fletcher* class destroyer in the South China Sea, the *Settebello* had a pretty nice ride as long as you didn't think too much about a cow wandering across the train tracks in front of you..

American tourists had a fairly evil reputation among Europeans at the time. We were viewed as being crude, uneducated, vulgar, rich boors. I have to admit that there was a certain amount of truth to this image, so I did my best to counter it, as a patriotic gesture. I wore jacket and tie most of the time, in muted colors, spoke reasonably fluent German and a smattering of French, and avoided (as best I could) giving the impression of being a young, obscenely rich American nabob. This was easy to do, as I had about zero money at the time.

Without modern instant communications and broad-band information, travel abroad contained more surprises for Americans than it does now. This trip was only 19 years after the end of World War II, and there were still a few lingering jolts.

In Munich, like all good tourists, I had to have a brew in the *Hofbrauhaus*, a kind of giant and ornate beer hall. That's where those Amazon barmaids heft a half-dozen liter beer steins in each hand. It's a huge place, laid out with picnic-style tables. A group of guys saw through my disguise, recognized that I was an American and invited me over. I wasn't exactly expecting a warm welcome-Munich had experienced 71 air raids during the war. But they were very friendly, and the conversations were far-ranging-including discussions of the war, which I had only the dimmest memories of, mostly revolving around air raid sirens in San Francisco.

Finally, the topic got around to Hitler, and one of the young men-who was too young to have been an actual fighter-said something like, "You know, if Hitler hadn't had 'ein Fehler in den Arsch' (a bug up the ass) about the Jews, we could have won the war." At least, that's what I

A local freight in Greece pulled by a tiny tank engine meanders through the countryside.

remember he said, but this was after about six beers.

The steam engine was to all intents and purposes dead in the United States, but in Central Europe, steam was alive and well, primarily because Europe had abundant coal resources, but oil was still wildly expensive. The steamers were mostly used for freight service but every

29

once in a while you could see a beat-up old teakettle dragging a commuter train to a low-rent suburb. Europe was rapidly expanding its electric railway system as an alternative to both coal and diesel, because the Alps had enormous hydroelectric potential. By the time of my second trip to Europe in '69, steam had croaked in Europe just as it had two decades before in America. But in '64, as is always the case in travel, occasionally you run into surprises. While my train was parked next to an engine servicing facility, I got a picture of a steam engine tender that was marked UNRRA. I found out much later that this stood for "United Nations Relief and Rehabilitation Administration," an organization that was set up during World War II in anticipation of an Allied victory, and from 1945-47 distributed more than $3 billion (mostly from the US) in supplies and services, primarily in Europe, for civilian rebuilding. This was in addition to the "official" Marshall Plan for European renewal that was developed by the US, and added up to an additional $17 billion. One wonders if Atilla the Hun had conquered Germany if he would have been as generous. One of their major areas of rehabilitation was in restoration of rail service which had essentially come to a stop by the end of the war, mostly because all the trains had been blown up and the track

UNRRA tender.

30

demolished. This old tender was what was left of a locomotive that had been supplied by UNRRA to help restore train service. I'm not sure exactly where the picture was taken, but I suspect Germany or Austria.

The further away you went from Western Europe, the more likely you were to find steam. Greek railroads were still primarily operated by very small steam locomotives.

The *Orient Express*. Ah, the images that name brings up. Countesses with lorgnettes leading armies of porters carrying trunks full of Chanel frocks. James Bond, undoubtedly having a dalliance with Pussy Galore on his way to Istanbul for the final showdown with Ivan Skavinsky Skivar. Baron de Rothschild, taking a little break from stomping the grapes for a bit of the waters on the Dalmatian coast.

Alas, when I took the *Direct Orient Express* from Milan to Athens, via Belgrade, every molecule of glamor had been surgically removed from the train itself, and what was left was a dismal Eastern European local train using equipment that in the U.S. would have been instantly condemned by at least 15 federal agencies. It was, however, part of the Eurailpass system, and there was one First Class car on the train. It was first class in the sense that chickens weren't running up and down the aisles, as they did in Second Class, and I don't want to think about Third Class. It was a long, slow trip, almost 18 hours as I remember, including an overnight.

The first time I had to use the bathroom, I staggered down the aisle toward a door marked "W.C.," opened it, and GAAAAAHHHHHH!!! was greeted by an odor the likes of which I have not, thank God, experienced since. It was like–no, dear reader, I will not even try, even though I might be able to come close. You might be enjoying a bagel or some such as you read, and I would not want to be responsible for your heaving your guts out. No, I will spare you that, but I will tell you what I saw when I entered the little room:

31

A hole in the floor. That's what the toilet was. A hole in the floor.

And with a wildly swaying car, booze flowing freely, and spicy middle-eastern food, you can, I think, visualize (odorize?) the scene.

The other thing I remember about the trip through the old Yugoslavia on the *Orient Express* was a vague sense of menace. It was not a particularly tense time in US-Soviet block relations–after all, the Limited Nuclear Test Ban Treaty had been signed just the year before, but I had started school at the beginning of the Red Menace era, and for all my waking memory, I had been taught about the Commies and the Russkies, and now, I was on a crappy train, it was midnight in Belgrade, and the Commie Yugoslav border guys, with their submachine guns, were *looking at my passport. Real hard.*

I had visions of prisons, sort of like the Turkish ones in *Midnight Express*. Huge, obscenely fat hairy prisoners wearing fezes, rubbing their greasy hands in anticipation of pawing me, while saliva slobbered down both sides of their toothless mouths.

Alas, although had it ended up that way it would have been a great story had I lived, the border guys were actually pretty nice and just wanted to cadge a couple of American cigarettes off me. It took me years to get rid of the image of that train, which is right up near the head of my list of 10 Worst Trains in the World.

After the summer months were up it was time to return home and begin the final phase of my graduate education, at the University of California, Davis. The return trip was made on another United States Lines ship, the *America*. She was the *United States'* older, smaller sister. She was launched in 1939, and almost immediately taken over by the U.S. Navy, renamed the *West Point*, and saw distinguished service in WWII as a troop transport. She had been designed by the same remarkable marine architect who designed her big sister, William Francis Gibbs. By 1964, she was getting long in the tooth for an ocean liner on the transatlantic run, and not long after my trip, she was sold to a Greek shipping line, and rebuilt to almost double the number of passengers carried, and used basically to carry immigrants from England to Australia. This service lasted for 14 more years. The rest of her career was sad, and unworthy of a ship that had served so well for so long.

Unfortunately, I don't remember a single thing about this trip back. In New York, another transcontinental train trip awaited (my sixth), and it was time to start my next three years in ornithology study at the University of California, Davis.

Chapter 3
The Davis Railroad Club[1]

The year after I left Berkeley (1963), the campus erupted with the Free Speech Movement riots. A couple of years after I finished my next academic stop, at San Francisco State, it too was torn with rioting and demonstrations. Had the administration at the University of California, Davis, known that I was apparently a harbinger of student unrest, I might not have been admitted to their grad school so easily in 1964. However, Davis didn't have any riots until 2004, and I'm sure my effect had worn off by that time. The town of Davis was an important SP junction and I immediately began an orgy of railroad photography.

Three major SP trains stopped there, the *City of San Francisco,* the *Cascade*, the *Shasta Daylight,* and two lesser ones, mail trains to Portland and Ogden. The former were pulled by the thrilling Alco PA passenger train diesel locomotives beloved by railfans, and the latter by the more mundane and common Electro Motive Diesel (EMD) FP-7s. In between taking pictures of trains, I taught four sections of an intro biology lab as a teaching assistant, and did a bit of bird research.

---

[1] Most of this chapter was originally printed in an article in the Southern Pacific Historic and Technical Society's magazine, "Trainline" in 2006. Reprinted with permission.

Alco PA locomotive pulling the *Shasta Daylight* out of Davis in the late '60s.

In the 1960s, students all over the United States were protesting the Vietnam War, racial injustice, and the plight of the poor. However, in Davis, a small group of dedicated student activists were also protesting something REALLY important-the abandonment of the *Shasta Daylight* by the Southern Pacific Railroad. I know, because I was one of them and I bear the memory of being hassled by SP railroad bulls (cops) as a badge of honor.

In 1964 I started at Davis as a Ph.D. candidate in Zoology. However, having been a railfan almost since before birth, I immediately decided to check out an announcement of a meeting of the Davis Railroad Club that was in the Davis student newspaper a few weeks after I arrived. It didn't have any specifics about what kind of group it was, however.

FP-7 picking up train orders at Davis.

There were no real surprises at the first meeting–a lot of pocket protectors and railroad badges in evidence. It was kind of interesting when two guys came very close to fisticuffs about what the piston diameter of an SP 4300 locomotive was. That was a bit esoteric even by my standards. But along with the hard-core "foamers" (a foamer is someone who foams at the mouth at the thought of a steam engine), there was a trio of students who were growing increasingly incensed by what appeared to be the high-handed tactics of the then-current chieftains of the SP, Chairman D.J. Russell, and President B.F. Biaggini, in their efforts to dump their passenger trains. Railroad officials then, as today, do not have first names. They are apparently born with initials only.

Although our Gang of Now Four was not as smitten with mechanical arcana as the foamers, we did share a curious vice that our British cousins called "trainspotting." Except we called it "keeping consists." A consist is the makeup of the cars in a train. Every time a passenger train pulled into Davis station, one or the other of us was down there with our spiral-bounds, listing the car numbers of each car in a train. I'm not exactly sure today WHY this was important, but it was; half the mileage on my automobile in Davis was expended getting from my apartment to the station. It may have had something to do with the fact that in the '50s, the SP had different paint schemes for the streamliners on each of their four major routes, and in some cases, for individual trains. Early on, the SP took a great deal of pride in keeping its trains together, but by the '60s they'd more or less given up, and the trains had a "rainbow" appearance; one car from the *Shasta Daylight*, one from the *Sunset Limited*, one from the *Lark*, etc. The result looked like something a six year old would cobble together with his Lionel cars–*very* low class.

By comparing notes with my new comrades in arms; Greg Thompson, Tom Matoff, and Glenn C. Lee, Jr., it quickly became clear that something fishy was going on. We knew where every passenger car on the SP system was at any one time, and with the attrition of trains that started in the '50s, there were plenty of modern, comfortable cars available for the surviving trains, yet we would regularly see living fossils from the '30s making up the bulk of a consist. There were a few other disturbing incidents we stumbled on that only a dedicated railfan would notice, and it wasn't long before we figured out what was happening.

Russell and Biaggini had apparently decided, like their equally far-sighted colleagues at the Pennsylvania and New York Central Railroads, that passenger trains were born-to-lose enterprises and even if they broke even on their expenses, the capital tied up in their operation could be much more profitably used elsewhere. Russell and Biaggini's measure as business prognosticators might be judged by the fact that other than among railfans, the now long-expired Southern Pacific Railroad has almost disappeared in the collective consciousness of Westerners, whereas the Union Pacific, which still operates big old-fashioned steam locomotives and railfan trips, is making a tidy profit and enjoys outstanding public relations.

R & B's problem was that being a quasi-public utility, the SP couldn't unilaterally dump its annoying "varnish" (passenger trains)-they had to request permission from the state Public Utilities Commission, and/or the federal Interstate Commerce Commission, which would then hold public hearings on the requests. The only ground they could use for abandonment was that the public had no demonstrated demand for the service, as shown by ridership. Ah, but what if some members of the old-fashioned public still stubbornly rode the trains despite the obvious superiority of car and airplane? Simple–make riding the trains such a dismal experience that no one in his right mind except a foamer who dreamed about Alco PA's would want to ride one.

It did not take long for the intrepid Davis Railroad Club Four to become students with a Mission. We would both alert the public about what was happening to "their" trains while they weren't looking, and would detective-fashion document the SP's nefarious deeds and thrash the villains in the cold light of daylight if they had the effrontery to request abandonment of one of our beloved trains.

Unfortunately, we got plenty of practice. SP passenger trains were being led to the knackers like chickens to Col. Sander's house. It didn't take us long to be rudely introduced to the reality of a "public" hearing. Train No. 40, the *Imperial*, from Los Angeles to El Paso was up for abandonment in 1967 after showing dismal ridership. The fact that it had actually been removed from the timetable a couple of years before may have had *something* to do with that. We had recorded the following conversation with an SP ticket clerk in Los Angeles:

"I'd like to go to El Paso tonight. What's the latest train that goes to El Paso?"
"That would be the *Sunset*. Leaves at 8:00 PM."
"I was thinking of something later, maybe around midnight?"
"No, we don't have anything like that."
"How about train No. 40 that leaves at 11:30 PM, usually from Track 4?"
"Oh, THAT train. Why didn't you say so?"

However, when we went on the stand to offer this (and other equally damning) testimony, the SP attorneys were all over us, asking about our professional qualifications as railroad experts. Of course we had none; we were just obnoxious, annoying, and probably Communistic students. The SP attorney having established our lack of credentials with little difficulty would turn to the examiner and say, "Objection. Incompetent." "Sustained," was the invariable reply.

It seemed that the ONLY thing a member of the public could testify to in these kangaroo-court hearings was that we rode the trains and requested their continuance. If we had a sound movie of a secret meeting between Russell and Biaggini in which Russell said, "B.F., why don't we sprinkle itching powder in the Pullman berths?" to which Biaggini would reply, "Great idea, D.J., and while we're at it, maybe we could double the number of cans of cockroaches we open in the dining cars," we would not have been able to offer it in evidence.

After a few of these extraordinarily frustrating experiences, Glenn, who turned out to be an absolute genius as a flack, suggested that the only way we were going to be heard was if there was an outraged public and press. Well, the public never did get outraged enough, which is why we have Amtrak, but the DRC generated enough press to make Brittany Spears embarrassed. We passed out handbills on the heavily used SF commuter trains (with the help of cooperative SP employees who looked the other way) that said "This train is DOOMED!" On another, a lampoon photo of Russell had a scowl that looked like a bulldog with an ulcer, so his picture fit nicely on the handbill. We staged what would today be called media events with the help of people like Tennessee Ernie Ford, Ray Bradbury, and Stan Freberg, who were all dedicated train riders. We leafleted the last departure of the *Lark*, the overnight Coast Line train from San Francisco to Los Angeles with a pamphlet that depicted SP management as a paunchy official aiming a shotgun at a helpless bird ("Hark Hark - no *Lark*?"). We know these events got the SP's goat, through contacts inside SP headquarters at 65 Market Street in San Francisco, and also judging from the heft and height of SP officials and their myrmidons who came to "chat" with us to persuade us to cease and desist. These heavies just didn't know what to make of us because we had no fear of lawsuits; we had no assets to lose. They were also smart enough to realize that with the anti-authoritarian climate of the time if they HAD tried anything nasty like trying to get us expelled from Davis, we would have made absolute mincemeat of them in the press.

Perhaps our greatest accomplishment was the production of a 156 page document outlining, in copious documented detail, SP's nefarious schemes. This was made in preparation for the *Shasta Daylight* abandonment hearings. Unfortunately, it was not admissible in evidence at the hearings, but established our credibility with the press. I dug my copy out a few weeks ago, and was dumbfounded. How did I ever finish grad school, with all the time that document required?

We never did win an abandonment case outright, but I like to think that we slowed The Octopus (Frank Norris' name for the SP in 1901) enough such that the SP hadn't scrapped or sold their passenger car fleet by the time Amtrak was formed. There are still dozens of former SP passenger cars yet running, most with private owners. The four of us went our separate ways after graduation, but the Railroad Club survived long enough to help establish UniTrans, UC Davis' public bus system. In a bit of long-forgotten minutiae, the initial bus lines were named after San Francisco streetcar routes.

In 1967, there was finally a reward for my efforts in behalf of the SP passenger trains. Although SP management was the mortal enemy of the Railroad Club (alright, to be fair, the Railroad Club members were more like annoying gnats to the bosses), the working stiffs

Cover of the DRC *Shasta Daylight* report.

and middle management were generally very supportive of us–after all, it was also their jobs that we were working to save.

As a result, we were given access to things that would be impossible to secure for

The "honorary steam locomotive," the Alco PA pulls out of Davis with the 24 cars of the *City of San Francisco* trailing behind.

"civilians." For example, I got a cab ride in the diesel locomotive most revered in America by railfans, the legendary Alco PA. I rode from Davis north to Winters where I got off, and hitched a ride back to Davis. I've had rides in many engine cabs since, and I've always been struck by how noisy and rough riding diesel engines are when you're up front. You'd have no idea as a passenger.

In August of '67, I somehow got the money to go to the annual meeting of the American Ornithologist's Union in Toronto. In a feat of bullshit I am still proud of, I wrote to the Santa Fe Railroad, said I was a Ph.D. student doing research on railroads for a transportation article, (sort of true), and could I get a cab pass to ride in the engine of the *Super Chief* through the famous Raton Pass in New Mexico and Colorado to study engine operations on severe grades? To my amazement, I duly received a pass.

A bit of a mystery cropped up while I was researching the trip for this chapter. The Santa Fe would not normally be the route of choice from northern California to Chicago, and the *Super Chief* would definitely not be the selection of the prune-faced accountant who was checking my expenses, as it leaves from Los Angeles. However, the Santa Fe's *San Francisco Chief* to Chicago doesn't go through Raton Pass. So I either started out on the *SF Chief*, and transferred over to the *Super Chief* someplace where they both made a stop, or

Modern Casey Jones.

went down to LA on the SP, and caught the *Super Chief* there. As a transfer would involve getting off the *SF Chief* at 1:45 am in a godforsaken place like Barstow, California, and then killing 18 hours until the *Super Chief* arrived, something tells me I went to LA. How I explained this to the prune-faced accountant I don't remember, but it was undoubtedly an example of a talent which has served me well in a long career of bending rules.

I got off the train in Albuquerque where there was a long stop, found the appropriate official, flashed my pass, and he sent me up to the head end of the train. The engineer gave me a "What on earth–?" look, but waved me up into the cab. It has long been the custom that engine crews carry something like a gym bag to carry their papers and small tools, so I had taken the precaution of putting my camera gear in such a satchel, rather than my normal camera bag, to give the impression that I knew what I was doing.

43

The Santa Fe locomotives were beautiful, clad in stainless steel with an ornate stylized "war bonnet" paint scheme. The inside of the cab was less attractive, being painted in the almost universal faded gas-chamber green I saw in most diesel engines. I know about gas-chamber green because one of my cousins was a doctor (family tradition) and worked at San Quentin prison, where he officiated at executions, and he told me about it.

Riding fireman on the *Super Chief.*

We slowly pulled out of Albuquerque, and the grade gradually steepened. The engineer was straight out of central casting; steely eyes, strong jaw. He wore a porkpie hat, which was *de rigeur* for engineers of the day. No striped cap. Pretty soon, you could hear, no *feel* the engines straining. When 6,000 hp strains, it gets your attention. I was somewhat astounded at how rough the ride was; once we cleared the pass onto flat land, and got up to 90+ mph, it was actually a little scary. I am embarrassed to admit that I was so stupefied by the ride that I didn't take any pictures going through the pass, but I did get a shot of a passing freight once we leveled off. I got off at Raton, and shambled back to my coach seat, ears still ringing. After that, the bird meetings were sort of anticlimactic.

All was not railroad politics and academics. In 1964, I took the Santa Fe's intrastate train in California, the *Golden Gate* between Richmond and LA. I seemed to have an evil cloud hanging over my head, because all too often, I'd ride a train, and it would be abandoned a short time later. That was the *Golden Gate's* fate in 1965. I took the Santa Fe again in that year, this time a vacation trip on the *San Francisco Chief* to Williams Junction in Arizona. There was then a transfer to a short connector train to the Grand Canyon. It was a quick walk from end of track to the edge of the canyon. This is one of the most stunning views in the world accessible by a train. After you get off your coach, you're just strolling along a little trail, and all of a sudden, you can almost hear the clash of cymbals, and the world drops away. This trip can be done on Amtrak today, and needs to be on everyone's train bucket list.

All four of us who led the Davis Railroad Club's war, albeit losing the battle against the SP, maintained a connection with rail for the rest of our professional lives. Greg is a retired professor of transportation planning and policy in Florida, Tom is a transportation consultant and manager still in the general Davis area, Glenn passed away a few years ago, but was a ferocious train, transit and ferry letter writer in Washington state. I made my living as professor of biology at the University of Rhode Island, but in retirement, I was the curator of the Rhode Island Railroad Museum, and Chairman of the Board of a preservationist volunteer group, the Friends of the Kingston Station. So the Davis Railroad Club may have been the most successful failure in railfandom.

Chapter 4

Land of the Starbucks; Home of the Grunge

In the late 1960s, the career path for greenhorn scientists experienced a rather dramatic change. Prior to that time, one got a Ph.D. in Advanced Nuclear Contemplation, or whatever, and then immediately applied for a job, typically as an assistant professor at a research university, where you did research, and in your spare time and expending as little energy as possible, you taught. Depending on the field, some folks went into government or industry jobs instead. But the "terminal" degree was the doctorate.

With the enormous injection of money by the federal government into the scientific enterprise during the space race, the academic marketplace started to look at additional time in which you did nothing but research as a desirable preparation for an academic job. Thus was born the "post-doctoral research fellowship," or post-doc.

When I finished my Ph.D. in 1967, post-docs were still not all that common, and not that many people took advantage of them. One of the reasons, on the surface, was economic. At the time, Ph.D. grad students were making about $2,900 a year. New assistant professors made about $11,000. The post-doc was right in the middle, at about $6,000. On the face of it, it wouldn't make sense to go the post-doc route, if you could be a prof at double the salary. But new assistant professors were considered to be adults. That meant you had to buy a house, wear a suit to work, drive something other than a junker, etc. So you really didn't have much more pocket money than you did before. But post-docs were still viewed socially as students, except now you were making twice as much as you were the year before. Looked good to me, so I started searching for a post-doc.

I found one at the University of Washington in Seattle, in the lab of a guy named Donald Farner. He was an ornithologist like I was, but he was like the General Motors of the bird business. He even had his own building. He was a member of the National Academy of Sciences, and seemed to know everybody in the world of high-level scientists. I later found out he was probably also a civilian spook for Naval Intelligence, and like clockwork, when he attended a conference in eastern Europe, three days after his return a guy from Washington with brown shiny shoes and a big briefcase dropped by for a visit. I figured that if I could impress him, his letter of recommendation would be worth gold. Turned out, it was.

Naturally, I took the train to Seattle from Davis, which was the junction of the SP's Shasta and Overland routes. In 1967, the sole Southern Pacific "streamliner" surviving on the Shasta route through California and Oregon was the *Cascade Limited* (usually referred to simply as the *Cascade*). Despite the heroic efforts of the Davis Railroad Club, the *Shasta Daylight* had been sent blindfolded to the wall in 1966. Perhaps the most spectacular part of the route was the view of Mount Shasta, the 14,000' "dormant" volcano that dominates northern California.

The *Cascade* in 1967 wasn't really a BAD train, even though it looked like hell from the outside, with cars from all over the system repainted in SP's new universal paint scheme of elephant gray, with an anemic blood red stripe. The interior was decently maintained, and despite the desires of SP's top management who wanted gruel to be the sole breakfast dish, Cheerios to be the entrée for lunch, and ground raccoon for dinner, food in the dining car was passable, but a far cry from the days when the SP chefs made fillet d'sole *marguery*, lamb cassoulet, chicken gumbo, and a version of beef Wellington, from scratch, on the train.

The *Cascade* ended at Portland, and a pool service run by the Great Northern, Northern Pacific, and Union Pacific handled trains between Portland and Seattle. The Union Pacific train terminated at Union Station in Seattle, and the other two ended up at King Street station.

It didn't take long for me to discover, once I settled in to my job, that I was probably living in the best place for a railfan in the United States in the years immediately before Amtrak. The three major railroads that served Seattle independently concluded that as long as they had to offer passenger train service, goddam it, it was gonna be GOOD service. So all the major long-distance trains pulling out of Seattle were nearly as gorgeous as they were in the golden '50s.

Also, with three major railroads terminating there, there were railyards, engine facilities, hidden tracks to explore, and endless photographic opportunities. My rented house was about 700 feet from the main Great Northern Line between Seattle and Vancouver, BC, and the Salmon Bay bascule bridge, so with my newly bought Topcon 35mm camera, I was

Salmon Bay bridge.

just as often trackside as lab bench side.

The rail situation in the late '60s in Seattle was terrific for the railfan, but there were also ominous winds of change in the air. The Boeing 747 made in Seattle would take its first flight in February, 1969. All the rail folks knew that ultimately the 747 would pose a huge challenge to long-distance rail travel, especially as seemed inevitably to happen, Gresham's Law (the bad drives out the good) started to apply, and air travel went from being comfortable for the rich, to abysmal but cheap for the poor.

There were actually four railroads that entered Seattle: Northern Pacific (NP), Great Northern (GN), Union Pacific (UP), and a regional line, the Spokane, Portland and Seattle (SP & S). All four were joined at the waist financially through a common ancestry in which the names J.P. Morgan, J.D. Rockefeller, E.H. Harriman, and J.J. Hill were instrumental. Functionally, the Union Pacific had split off many years before. A 5th line, the Chicago, Burlington and Quincy (Burlington) was owned by the same interests, and operationally was tied to the GN and NP by providing their connection to Chicago.

All the lines had separate managements, but the president of the Burlington during the mid-'60s was a man named Louis Menk. Rather surprisingly, considering the enormous impact he had on northwest railroads, he has faded into near obscurity–a recent Google search turned up relatively few mentions. No question about it, he was a very capable railroad executive, but he had two bugs in his ear. The first said that one big railroad is better than two smaller railroads. The second said that passenger trains could never be made profitable, and should take a trip down the memory hole. This put him in the category of Great Satan to northwest railfans.

However, his *methodology* was nothing like the slimy/creepy practices of SP management. He didn't believe in driving passengers away by lousy service. He accomplished his first objective of consolidation by presiding over the merger of the GN, NP, and Burlington in 1970, and in that same year, Amtrak solved his second problem for him by taking over most American passenger trains. What this meant for the railfan (yours truly) in Seattle was that 1967-1969 was a golden period of huge changes that were fascinating to observe and document.

In 1967, the GN and NP's trains were still completely separate and competing. They duked it out on who had the best service to Chicago (the NP's *North Coast Limited* still had stewardesses and Raymond Loewy designed interiors), and food service. I rode the GN's premier train, the

49

Empire Builder, more often than the *North Coast*, and I must admit I salivate a little when I think about the *Builder*'s diner.

The GN was a pioneer in the "locovore" concept. Eastbound, for dinner on the first night out of Seattle, you might start with chowder made from geoduck clams, and then maybe fresh King or Cohoe salmon, depending on the season, or a San Francisco style cioppino. Second day out, the dining car would restock in Montana, and the specialty was locally raised and processed beef, either simple like a steak, or a ragoût of beef. Going the other direction out of Chicago, first night out you'd have a lake whitefish. Naturally, all breads and pastries were baked on board. Just like Amtrak, eh?

The paint schemes of the competing trains were quite different. The GN had an orange and dark green stripe design, the colors separated by narrow yellow strips. The NP's scheme was more subtle–a two tone green separated by white stripes. However, in 1967, the GN switched

Rainbow train.

over to a simplified "Big Sky Blue" scheme. The trains were repainted one car at a time, so we began to see "rainbow" trains. To those of us in the railfan community, this was an ominous sign–in the "old days" an entire set of cars would be taken out of service during a slow time of the year for repainting, so to see a train of miscellaneous colors was a sign that management had given up on quality.

Then in 1970, Lou Menk engineered the merger of the BN, NP, and CB & Q, into the "Burlington Northern" (BN) and very quickly, there was a BN paint scheme that looked very much like the "Big Sky Blue" scheme, substituting a medium green for the blue. Now the "rainbow" trains would often have three different paint schemes on the cars.

Despite all the corporate turmoil, the pre-BN roads were very helpful to railfans. They frequently ran special excursion trains on their own. One memorable trip was on the NP to Stampede Pass, the NP's historic entrance to the Puget Sound area from the east. The trip was in winter, and the train stopped at the top of the pass to let the kids out to throw snowballs.

There was also a very active local chapter of the National Railway Historical Society. This group owned a couple of streamlined passenger cars which could be attached to the back of a regular train, either freight or passenger. Some of these trips could be enjoyed by the general public and

Fantrip to Stampede Pass.

were widely advertised. They often served as fundraisers.

Other trips, however, were more, ah, *specialized*, and of primary interest to individuals bordering on the extreme end of the railfan spectrum. One such trip was on the main SP & S tracks from Seattle to Portland, then following the NP up the Columbia River to Wishram, Washington. At Wishram, the Columbia River was crossed, and the NRHS car was fastened to the "Bend Local" from Wishram to Bend, Oregon, following the Deschutes River canyon line of the old Oregon Trunk Railroad.

This train was what was called in the old days a "mixed." That is, it was mostly freight cars, but with an antique passenger car or two tacked on to serve the locals who lived in remote areas. These trains had timetables, but they were honored more in the breach than the observance. The Deschutes River had some of the best fishing in the Northwest, and the only way to get to its central portion was by canoe, or the train. The train left Wishram at 1 AM, sort of, and arrived in Bend at 7:00 AM, more or less. Going the other way, it left Bend at about 7:00 PM and got into Wishram around midnight. So, a scenic run it was not.

However, it catered royally to the needs of the fishermen. All they had to do is tell the conductor of the train where they wanted to get off, he'd stop the train, and do a pickup a couple of days later. How did the crew know where the fishermen would be, given that the whole run was done at night? He'd just build a fire next to the tracks, the engineer would see it, and while he was putting the fire out, they'd stop the train.

The train was a railfan's paradise. You could ride in the engine if you wanted, or in the cars that were regularly assigned to the train. One was a '20s coach, the other was a combination coach-baggage car with large sliding doors. The train crew had somehow gotten hold of a spotlight off a WWII destroyer, and rigged it in a sling in one of the door openings. So if you wanted to ride in the baggage car, the conductor would illuminate points of interest along the way. We also noted that there was a nice

Winchester 30-'06 bolt action rifle mounted in a scabbard next to the light. When we were sworn to secrecy, the crew revealed that during hunting season, they would jacklight deer from the train. Since they worked at night, and slept during the day, after all, when *could* they hunt?

At Bend, we switched over to one of the few municipally owned railroads in the United States, the City of Prineville Railroad. It had been built as a result of a snub and an opportunity. When a railroad was built north to south in central Oregon, Prineville hoped it would be on the route, to service its burgeoning lumber mill business. Alas, the railroad decided to go to Bend, about 30 miles away. We don't know whether Prineville simply pissed the railroad off, or failed to pay enough *scarole*, as we Rhode Islanders say, but the normal outcome when a town in the boonies was bypassed was a slow, but inevitable death. However, in 1918 the gutsy town fathers decided to build a railroad branchline using town money.

When we visited Prineville in the late '60s, the town and the railroad were not exactly *thriving*, but they were surviving. The experience was good for me in one respect, though. I resolved that I would never, ever, want to reside in a place like Prineville, even

Oregon Trunk Railroad depot in Bend, Oregon.

53

Bend local in the Deschutes River canyon. Note the baggage door in the combination car just forward of the car in the foreground.

though it was only 121 miles from the nearest major city, Eugene. A Big Mac run distance for a Texan.

On the way back home; another lucky find. In one of the yards near Wishram, I discovered an operating, but relatively rare Alco FA freight diesel locomotive. Behind it, on a flatcar, was the Northern Pacific's first engine, the *Minetonka*, dating from the 1870s. It was kind of a nomad, traveling around the NP system whenever they needed a little good publicity–kids loved it, sort of like *Thomas the Tank Engine*.

Although I was working very hard in the lab, there seemed to be a lot of time for railroad and ship side trips. It was just a short

Alco FA near Wishram, on the bank of the Columbia River.

run on one of the GN's *Internationals* along the spectacular Puget Sound run to Vancouver, and Victoria, BC. The *Princess Marguerite II* was a lovely little "miniature ocean liner" that ran on the Seattle-Vancouver run. Steam logging operations on the Olympic Peninsula had pretty much stopped by the early '60s, but you could still see log trains hauling enormous logs, and the occasional old abandoned steam locomotive.

A car trip to eastern Washington revealed a railroad

Princess Marguerite en route to Vancouver from Seattle.

treasure. The Chicago, Milwaukee, St. Paul, and Pacific Railroad ("Milwaukee") had the longest stretch of electrified track in the United States, much of it in Washington State. In the mid-'60s, freight trains were still being pulled over the Bitterroot and Cascade mountains by enormous electric locomotives. Much of the line was not easily accessible by car, but at Beverly, a small-a very small-town on the bank of the Columbia River, there was a tiny rail yard where helper engines were stored in case they were needed for heavy trains going to Seattle. After a long trip from Seattle, and a drop down off the Cascades, there they were; a line of the Milwaukee's "Box Cab" electrics, looking like brontosauruses standing in front of an ATM. I got there just in time-electric service ended in the early '70s, and the line itself was abandoned in 1980. Today, the right-of-way is a hiking trail.

Milwaukee Road electrics at Beverly, Washington .

I had my first plane ride when I was staying in Seattle. I'd barely settled in, when I received word from San Francisco that my father had passed away, and I needed to get home pronto. There wasn't really time to take the train down, so I asked my travel agent (everybody used travel agents in those days) to book me a flight to The City. It was getting close to Christmas, but she found a spot.

I had no idea what to expect. I wore a jacket and tie, because, well, that was simply something that *one did* while traveling. I suppose I was also a little chicken; worldwide, there had been 80 commercial airline crashes with fatalities in 1967, including eight with more than 50 deaths, but I think it was more that I was afraid of making some kind of *faux pas* because I didn't know the drill. I was Master and Commander aboard a train, but on United Flight XXX, I was just another yokel.

It was about an hour and a half flight from Seattle to San Francisco in a Boeing 720, over the Cascades. I had heard that it was often bumpy over the Cascade mountains, but I wasn't sure what, exactly, "bumpy" meant. Like going over a speed bump? Or a screaming, passengers-bouncing-off-the roof descent into the maw of hell?

Well, it was actually pretty smooth, and they served lunch. A small green salad, a *filet mignon*, fresh steamed vegetables, some nice *petits fours*, and a complementary split of California cabernet, a Beaulieu, as I recall. And this was in coach. So far, so good.

For what happened next, you need to know that the way they space airliners coming into an airport has changed dramatically since those days. Now, they can tell exactly how long a trip will take, so they hold the plane on the ground until there's exactly enough time to make the destination, with no waiting at the other end.

That precision was not there in the old days, so planes were landed at a destination airport first-come, first-served. New planes arriving in the airport area were put in a "stack" of airplanes all circling on top of each other, 1,000 vertical feet apart. There might be 12-15 airliners in the stack on a busy day. When a runway became available, the bottom plane would drop off, and everybody else would descend 1,000 feet.

San Francisco NEVER has convective weather (thunderstorms). Well, hardly ever. The stack was always in the same place relative to the ground, and just my luck, the stack was right in the middle of one of those thunderstorms San Francisco never gets.

The plane pitched up. It pitched down. It rolled 45 degrees to the right. Then to the left. A sickening drop was immediately followed by a berserker up elevator ride. The plane was hit by lightning. The cabin lights went out. Passengers were crying. Passengers were praying. I was too busy puking to do either.

The plane finally landed, accompanied by the obligatory round of applause for the pilot. I got myself assembled, and suddenly realized that I might be about to commit one of those *faux pas* I had so dreaded. What do you do with the, ah, occupied airsick bag? It didn't seem right to just LEAVE it there. So I carefully folded over the top, and handed it to the stewardess who was standing by the exit. She was very gracious about it, considering that my face was a ghastly shade of puce green. As a way of trying to explain myself, I said, "Miss, this was my first flight in an airplane. Is flying always like this?" She smiled merrily, and said, "Oh, Sir, sometimes it's MUCH worse than this!"

Swell.

A couple of days later it was time to go home. After my First Flight, I was tempted to turn in the return part of my air ticket, and take the train back, but I would have lost too much money. So, once again, I found myself strapped in an airplane, sort of like you are in the electric chair, waiting for takeoff.

At San Francisco airport, with a north wind, planes headed for the Pacific Northwest use runway 28, the same strip that the Asiana airplane that crashed in 2013 was trying to reach. The runway points in the general direction of San Bruno Mountain in South San Francisco, where I had collected lizards and salamanders as a kid. If you were standing on the south side of the mountain, when a plane took off from 28, it almost looked like it was aimed at your forehead, but of course, by the time it got to the mountain, it was thousands of feet overhead.

We taxied out to the end of the runway, the engines spooled up, there was a tremendous noise, and we barreled down the runway like a top fuel dragster. The plane rotated, and started to climb like a homesick angel. This was kinda fun! Then–. Dead silence.

As the plane started to drop and head straight toward San Bruno Mountain, I was ready to scream, "We're all going to die!" but I looked around and saw that my fellow travelers were non-plussed, and beginning to read their in-flight magazines. Then, I could hear the engines once more, and it seemed like we started to climb again.

I later found out what happened. The early Boeing 4-engine jets had a power-assist system for takeoffs that was called "water injection." It acted kind of like an afterburner on a military jet. You got a tremendous increase in sound level and about 20% more power. It was very wasteful of fuel, so they shut it off as soon as the plane got to about 1,000 feet. The noise had been SO loud that people were temporarily deafened, and when they shut the injection off, you couldn't hear the engines any more. The plane stopped climbing as fast, but it *felt* like the plane was dropping.

I didn't actually wet my pants, but I didn't get on another plane for 5 years. Ironically, many years later, I got a pilot's license, and became a volunteer search and rescue pilot for the Civil Air Patrol. But I didn't like flying commercial until I discovered the miraculous invention for frequent travelers called the Upgrade in the '80s. However, now that free upgrades for non-rich, non-frequent flyers are as rare as the Sumatran Rhinoceros, I have resumed my loathing for commercial flight.

My two years in Seattle went by with astonishing speed, and although I would have loved to continue as a regular faculty member at University of Washington, there were no openings. Finally, in the spring of 1969, I heard about a regular faculty job at the University of Rhode Island. My total knowledge about Rhode Island at the time can be easily summarized–the state is small. I officially finished up at Washington in June, but didn't have to start at Rhode Island until the week before Labor Day. Clearly, that called for another trip to Europe over the summer before I would be forced to become an adult with a real job at the age of 29.

Chapter 5

Les Trains de l'Europe: Deuxième Voyage

The trip to Europe in '69 followed the same pattern as the previous one in '64, but differed in several significant ways. It was shorter and covered fewer countries, but over the pond and back were again by ship. As I was about to become gainfully employed, there was more disposable income. Still, one of the main objectives was a lot of train riding.

QE 2 taking on fuel in New York harbor at Pier 90.

The voyage over was on the brand-new *Queen Elizabeth 2*. I mean *really* brand new; it was her maiden eastbound. The quarters were still in tourist class, but a lot had happened to the transatlantic travel business in the 5 years between my European trip 1 and trip 2.

Transatlantic jet service was introduced in the late 1950s, and several iterations of the Boeing 707 and Douglas DC-8 started packing the passengers in. The 707 was originally configured with 5-abreast seating, but that nicety was soon sacrificed to the beancounters. The Boeing 747 would be commercially introduced in 1970, and the steamship companies could read the handwriting on the wall. The airlines, sooner or later, were going to suck up all the bargain travelers, and the end of that road we can see today; airliners now are buses with wings. All they need is a big dog painted on the side. For the ship lines, that meant "tourist" would have to be upgraded to cater to what might later be called the "yuppie" passenger; not a WHOLE lot of disposable income, but elevated tastes and expectations.

It was in the dining rooms that this really showed up. There was nothing wrong with tourist dining on the earlier ships, but the *QE 2* was clearly several notches above. On the transatlantic liners of the day, what is today called "fixed" dining was the absolute rule. You were assigned the same table and table companions for the whole voyage, and had the same waiter. It was very difficult to change once the original assignment was made.

So what happened if one of your table companions had a high whiney voice, another smelled bad, a third was a funeral director, and the fourth was an auditor for the IRS? Weeeelll, that's where a little travel savvy came in. When you made your initial reservation, you explained to the headwaiter that you were a man of wealth and taste, and would GREATLY appreciate (quietly slipping the $20 into his discretely available palm) some interesting companions.

My tablemates were a delightful Swiss lady who unbelievably spoke no English, a pair of (in retrospect) gay doctors, and a wholly unique individual who it was my honor, pleasure, and bemusement eventually to know. He was English, his name was John Bunyan, and he was a lineal descendent of THE John Bunyan of *Pilgrim's Progress* fame. He was a bit portly, wore pince-nez glasses, and was a chain smoker. It was apparently against his philosophical principles to flick the ash off the end of his cigarette, so as his fag burned down, his companions would stare in horrified fascination waiting for the inch-long ash to drop off onto his ample shirt front. His voice was deep, booming, and a cross between John Cleese and Winston Churchill. By profession, he was an oral surgeon, but he was of independent means, a scientist, medical engineer, and a past president of the Royal Microscopical Society. He was interested in burn therapy as a result of his exposure to some of the horrible injuries the Brits suffered during WWII. Bizarrely, he LOVED Texas, and had spent a lot of time in the research labs of the University of Texas medical school. If you want to hear something truly strange, listen to a man whose native dialect is Oxford English trying to do a Texas drawl, dear boy. Or y'all, dear boy.

Perhaps the most striking thing about John was that he knew everybody. Anybody connected with Arthur Conan Doyle or Sherlock Holmes; he knew. Half the famous American or British scientists I was familiar with; he knew. When he found out I was going to Rhode Island, he said I must look up Dr. Howard Browne, a navy doctor and Sherlock Holmes buff in Newport. I did, and we have been friends for 40 years.

Over dinner, somehow the topic turned to microscopes. He mentioned that he collected them, and invited me to drop by his home near the cliffs of Dover to see them. I couldn't make it on this trip, but I took him up on his offer a few years later. He was a widower by this time, and lived in a lovely little cottage near the cliffs. He had a housekeeper, but she couldn't keep up with the cigarette ashes. He had microscopes everywhere; some in cases, some just sitting on tables, a thin film of ash giving each of them a dusky patina. He pointed out one fairly commonplace looking one, and told me that it had belonged to Sir Alexander Fleming, when he had discovered penicillin in the '20s. He then said. "I've got a Leeuwenhoek here someplace. Let me see if I can find it." He then started rummaging through a drawer.

63

A Leeuwenhoek ?!? Antonie van Leeuenhoek was a Dutchman who invented the microscope in the 1600's. He was probably the first man to actually see bacteria and cells. Only 9 of his original microscopes are known to have survived. And John had one of them in a drawer. After rooting around, John exclaimed, "Ah! Here it is. Come outside, dear boy, and let's look at something."

Leeuwenhoek's microscope looked nothing like modern 'scopes. It was a tiny thing; a few pieces of brass, a screw, and a minuscule lens. We went out into his garden, where it was a beautiful sunny afternoon. John pulled a leaf off a shrub, scratched it with his fingernail, and affixed it to the 'scope. "Take a look at this," he said, handing it to me. At first, all I saw was a green blur, but then I twisted the screw a bit, and my God! Cells jumped out. I realized with awe that I might be looking through the first instrument with which man ever saw cells. I was too dumbstruck to say anything but, "Thank you!"

QE2 flying the two black balls.

Midway through this first return voyage of the *QE 2*, we were having lunch, when we gradually became aware that things seemed to be quieter than usual, and the ship was developing a bit of a roll. Nothing alarming, it was a quiet sea, but definitely not normal. After about 15 minutes, there was an announcement that for some reason, the ship had lost propulsion power and headway, and we were (temporarily) adrift. I'm sure the word "adrift" was not used, but I don't remember what the non-alarming weasel substitute was. There was no estimate when we

64

would be underway again. I finished lunch, got my camera and went topside to see if there was anything to see. Indeed there was. The crew was hoisting two large black balls up the flag mast. Two black balls is the international flag signal for "vessel not under command." There never was an announcement about what happened, but after a couple of hours, the black balls came down, and we were underway again. Kind of made you appreciate the lifeboat drills.

On this trip, there was scheduled to be more travel in the UK than before, and Ireland was on the itinerary. The *QE2* debarked in Southhampton, there were a couple of days in London, then it was off to the Emerald Isle.

Night train from Holyhead.

There are two ways to get to Ireland, both a combination of rail and ferry. I don't have a written record of the itinerary I took, but later pieced it together from the photographs of the trip that survive. Evidently, it was a loop trip, starting with the northern route. The first leg went from London northwesterly up through Crewe, and then west following the coast of northern Wales to the port of Holyhead. The portion of the line between Chester and Holyhead fairly reeks with railroad history, and I was to return many years later to wallow in it. I didn't know it at the time, but the train passed over one of the most famous bridges in railway engineering history, Robert Stephenson's Brittania Tubular Bridge crossing the Menai Straights between the mainland of Wales and Anglesey. The bridge was opened in 1850, and remained in use until the year following this trip, when it was destroyed by an accidentally started fire. Found on this line is the small rural community of Llanfairpwllgwyngyllgogerychwyrndrobwllllantysiliogogogoch (copy editor: please check spelling. Hahaha.) which actually has a train station.

Today, train times and ferry times are much faster than they were then, but it was an overnight trip in the late sixties, and it was at Holyhead that I got one of my favorite train crew pictures. From Holyhead, the ferry sails across the Irish Sea to a port near Dublin with the unpronounceable Gaelic name of Dun Laoghire.

Dublin should be on everyone's must-see list. It is charming, cosmopolitan, and small enough to be manageable. It has two main train stations. At the time of my stay, it also had a most peculiar institution- The *Radio Train*.

The *Radio Train* was a rolling party. It was mostly bar cars, and in one of the cars there was a DJ who staged interviews, played music, and engaged in patter with the passengers. There were loudspeakers in each of the cars so it was like–listening to the radio. I don't know if they actually broadcast from the train-that would have

Radio Train.

been a bit of a stretch for the technology of the day. There were no fixed destinations but it typically ran to various tourist locales on different days of the week. The service ran for 30 years, ending in the late '70s. It was briefly revived in 2009. I believe I took it to the Lakes of Killarney.

Station at Cork.

As I was about to launch a career as a college professor, naturally, I had to kiss the Blarney Stone at Blarney Castle, to develop my skills as a bullshit artist. Then as now, you had to crawl through a hole in the parapet atop a 70' high wall, bend over backwards, and hang with your head down over the edge of the wall to smack the stone. One of the castle workers who you had tipped generously in advance held you by the ankles to prevent you from falling head first and screaming to certain and undignified death. So it was something you really had to want to do. In today's litigious society, I imagine they wipe the stone down with Handi-Wipes between bussers, but such niceties were unknown in the late '60s, so you tried not to think of the vile and loathsome diseases the guy before you left on the rock from his rotting and pustulent lips.

Blarney was apparently about as far as I got in Ireland, because when I look at the photos of the rest of the trip, they suggested that I had made a counter-clockwise circle, changing trains at the beautiful station in Cork and ending at the main southern cross-Irish Sea port, Rosslare. From Rosslare, a three hour ferry ride takes you to Fishguard in south-west Wales, and then from there, you take a train back to London.

From London, it was the channel ferry across the English Channel, and then the ferry train to Paris. I won't say much about the French portion of the trip, because its purpose was gastronomic rather than railfanning. I had a head start on being a restaurant nut by growing up in San Francisco, where a crappy restaurant lasts about a month because there is so much excellent competition. I was not a stranger to good food. My mother was an excellent cook and one of my elementary school classmate's father owned *Alioto's*, the still-operating Fisherman's Wharf institution, and another owned one of the better Chinatown restaurants. For my high school graduation dinner my parents took me to *Ernie's*, where Jimmy Stewart took Kim Novak in Hitchcock's *Vertigo*. But, to paraphrase Al Jolson in *The Jazz Singer*, I hadn't seen nothin' yet. When I went to Seattle in the late '60s its fortunes were rising as fast as mine were, excellent restaurants were abundant and affordable, and by the time I left the northwest for this European trip in 1969, I was a confirmed "foodie."

The road between Paris and Lyon was known as the *Route de la Gastronomie* because there were so many Michelin starred restaurants along the way. The final destination for me was *Restaurant La Pyramide* in Vienne, outside Lyon. This was generally considered to be the best restaurant in the world at the time, largely due to the efforts of its founder, Chef Fernand Point, who basically established modern French cooking. Point was an enormous man, pushing 300 pounds, and once said about meeting a new chef, "If he is thin, I shall probably dine poorly." Makes sense.

I was more than a little intimidated by the prospect of having lunch at a restaurant whose usual customers were kings, emperors, presidents, generals, movie stars and titans of industry. However, I had studied the menu in advance, had (barely) the price of the meal, and had been in enough good restaurants to know the drill.

Once again, I discovered that in the great restaurants of the world, if you can show you know and understand outstanding food, you'll get excellent service no matter who you are. The service was quiet, unostentatious, and anticipated desires before they were expressed. No "Is everything to your satisfaction?" No hovering. Monsieur Vincent, the *maitre d'* made me feel like Clark Gable, or the Shah of Iran, who had been previous customers.

"Était-ce le meilleur repas de votre vie ou quoi?"

The lunch was 12 courses, each more spectacular than the one before. There were flavors and combinations I'd never tasted, and I was totally mystified as to how they were made–which is as it should be in a first class eaterie. It was 3 hours of pure bliss. Unfortunately, it was also about 4,000 calories worth of food, which started to bite back about an hour after the meal, but in a little country bar I fortunately discovered a wonderful treatment for too much pleasure at the table, an intensely bitter Italian *digestif* called Fernet-Branca. The taste is difficult to describe, kind of a mixture of aspirin, iodine, quinine, dead cat, skunk, rat puke, land fill, and toejam. I think it worked primarily in a moral sense. The taste is your punishment for overindulging, and then it gives you redemption. Wonderful stuff.

As a new Assistant Professor, I could afford (barely) this world class meal. Today, one unassuming appetizer at *La Pyramide* costs more than the entire meal with a pair of outstanding wines did then. Today's middle class folks like I was back in the day, can't come even close to being able to afford these modest luxuries, even with dual incomes. The Assistant Professors who replaced me when I retired in 2010 couldn't dream of leading the life I did four decades prior (unless, or course, they had independent means, which I didn't). Farewell, Middle Class; it was a great ride while it lasted.

After the drive back to Paris, and the terror-filled experience of driving in competition with crazed Parisian taxi drivers across the eight lanes of the Champs Elysees to return the rental car, it was off to Switzerland, and trains again.

My first trip to Switzerland in '64 concentrated mostly on the railroads around Lake Geneva. I had been tasked to visit one of my grandmother's old friends from Korea, who now lived in a little lakeside town named Vevey, where one of her neighbors was Charlie Chaplin. This second trip was focused more on the mountain railroads in the general area of

Interlaken.

From Lausanne, on Lake Geneva, I took one of the Simplon Tunnel

Train yard in Zermatt.

route trains that run through the increasingly spectacular and narrowing Valais valley to the junction town of Brig. As you approach Brig, the Loëtschberg line from Interlaken descends into the valley from the north, with some spectacular viaducts along the way . At Brig, there is a change from the Swiss Federal standard gauge train to a narrow gauge cog railroad running from Brig to Zermatt. The Zermatt Bahn is not what you usually think of as a "cog railroad" like the one on Mount Washington. Rather, it looks like a regular railroad . The tracks look like regular tracks until the grade pitches up so much that the wheels would begin to slip, and then a toothed rack appears between the rails, and the train is no longer powered by the adhesion between wheels and rails, but by a motor-driven gear (cog) in the engine that meshes with the toothed rack.

Matterhorn from Gornergrat. The railroad is at lower right.

The town of Zermatt is an oddity. There are no internal combustion cars permitted. The central touristic feature is Matterhorn peak, which from the town is a jaw-dropping sight. There is an extensive network of ski lifts and gondolas surrounding the town for skiing in winter, but for the rail fan there is a traditional cog railroad, the Gornergrat Bahn, which climbs a vertical elevation of 4,000 feet up the Gornergrat ridge to a plateau. From there, if one is so inclined, one may walk/climb to the top of the Matterhorn, which is about 7 miles, and another 4,000 vertical feet to the top.

From Zermatt, I doubled back in the direction of Bern on the Loëtschberg line to Spietz, then went past Interlaken to Brienz, a lovely little town on Lake Brienz. Not that Brienz isn't a charming place, but the main reason people go there is to ride on the Brienz Rothorn Bahn, Europe's only all-steam mountain railroad. Although it is not the steepest cog railroad in the world, it is soil-your-pants steep, as it clings to the very edge of a

"Daddy, I want one of these for Christmas."

1,000' cliff, while ascending a 25% grade (compared to about 2% for a regular railroad). Now, I love the Mount Washington Cog Railroad in New Hampshire, and have ridden it many times, but its steam locomotives look like they were cobbled together from parts found at the Junkyard Dog Auto Salvage Yard, whereas the parts on the Brienz' locos look like they're stamped "Rolex." But hey, it's Switzerland.

After Brienz it was a short trip back to Interlaken, where I started the three-railroad hop to the most spectacular railroad destination I've ever

The Eiger.

been to; the Jungfraujoch, a mountain col between the Mönch and Jungfrau peaks in the Bernese Oberland mountains.

From Interlaken, one must change trains twice before boarding the Jungfraujoch Bahn at Kleine Scheidegg, an interchange point at the foot of the mountain complex. For you Clint Eastwood fans, the *Eiger Sanction* was shot on location in the town of Kleine Scheidegg, and Clint himself did a lot of his own climbing.

The ride from Kleine Scheidegg station is fairly short and out in the open. At the base of the massif, the track dives into a four mile long tunnel that climbs just inside the cliff face of the Eiger and Mönch. At two locations along the way there is a "window" where the train stops and you can get off and get the same view as an Alpine climber, without any risk to your life, but considerable risk to your wallet (the trip is expensive). At the top at a little over 11,000 feet, you get off, have a stroll around the observation deck, and marvel at the ingenuity and bravery of the engineers and workers who built this astounding railroad.

After that, things were a bit of an anticlimax until the voyage home on the SS *France*. The *France* was only two years old when I took her back

74

to New York, and she still had the fresh paint smell. She was made to an entirely different design philosophy than the vessel I took eastbound on the '64 trip, the *United States*. The *United States* was all about speed, strength, and efficiency (sort of like America in those days, come to think about it). The *France* was designed around style, grace, and elegance, sort of like France used to be, too.

One of the first things most people think about "France" is "food." It was there that the *SS France* excelled, even in tourist class. The great restaurants, including the ones on the *France* all share certain characteristics. First is *precision*. Everything is where it should be, when it should be. Second is *effortlessness*. They make incredibly difficult things look like even you could do them-until you think about it a little or actually try to do them. Finally, there is *respect for knowledge*. Even if you are wearing ratty old unstylish professor clothes, if you ask the *maitre d'* thoughtful, considered questions, you can get an invitation to the kitchen. I think it was on the *France* that I began to recognize these observations as truth.

A little extra *frisson* was added in mid-voyage when we ran into a hurricane square-on. There was more pitching than rolling, and they had to put the little rails around the tables in the dining room for the few hardy luncheon goers, but I don't remember it as being particularly *scary*. Impressive, yes. There was a tourist-class bar where you could look out over the foredeck, and every once in a while, the tip of the bow would dip below sea level, and an enormous wave would spray over the bridge. Fortunately, *The Poseidon Adventure* had not yet come out, so unpleasant possibilities did not suggest themselves.

After about 5 days of memory-making meals, it was time to get off at New York, and take a Penn Central train to what would be my professional home for the next 40+ years, Kingston, Rhode Island. Amtrak had a year to go before taking over America's passenger trains, and Penn Central, or the part of it that used to be the New York, New Haven, and Hartford, was still running the trains between Manhattan and

Rhode Island. Back in my Davis grad student days, I had thought the SP had run its trains into the ground, but--. This Penn Central train should have had a sign on it saying, "Another shipment of contented cows for America's tables." As I got off the rusted coach and stepped on to the cracked platform at Kingston, an old unpleasant ditty ran through my mind:

> As I sat there, weak and weary,
> A small voice came, bright and cheery.
> "Buck up," it said. "Things could be worse."
> Sure enough, things got worse.

Penn Central train creaking and rattling into Kingston, Rhode Island.

Chapter 6
Little Rhody

The shock of going in five days from the dining rooms of the SS *France* to Giro's Pizza, which was the best restaurant convenient to my new employer, the University of Rhode Island, was profound. I had discovered as many people have, that there are certain things about a new job that an employer fails to mention in the hiring interview. Silly me, I didn't realize that the University of Rhode Island was in a rural area. I figured that being really close (in California terms) to New York and Boston, it must be in an urban setting, maybe like Berkeley. I was also told that I would be teaching a "large introductory biology class." Large, of course, is a relative term, but in this case it meant almost 1,000 reluctant non-science students in one auditorium. Somehow the fact that the previous instructor was nearing candidacy for assisted living and had allowed almost unlimited cheating for years escaped mention. So you can imagine the screams of rage when the students took their first exam with me and discovered to their horror that they hadn't already seen the questions, which under the previous professor had been collected and stored in dorm and fraternity files. There were actually petitions to the chair of the department complaining about this base unfairness.

There were enormous differences between the coasts in the late '60s, and I have to admit I now miss the local eccentricities which have mostly been lost in the wave of homogenization that started with national news broadcasters who had had their regional accents surgically removed before joining the networks. Just the concept of "distance" in Rhode Island was very different from what I grew up with on the West Coast.

In California you'd drive a hundred miles for a really good hamburger. In Seattle, a nice weekend sightseeing trip might be a 500-600 mile round trip. So, now that I was in New England, after I had a couple of months of settling in I figured it was time to explore the cradle of our democracy up in Massachusetts. Shot heard around the world. Lexington and Concord.

A glance at the map revealed that Concord was only 67 miles from Kingston as the crow flies. Piece of cake. Nice lunch trip. Leave maybe around 11, have lunch, check out the sights, be back around 3-4.

Yeah, right.

Getting to Concord by car meant traveling on Route 128 in Massachusetts, which was a lot more terrifying then than it is now, but it still is white-knuckle territory if you're not used to it. The trip took over double the time that I had figured. It also introduced me to Massachusetts drivers, who were legendary for aggressiveness. I hadn't realized that someone could flip you the bird while simultaneously cutting you off.

That trip marked the beginning of my abandonment of "pleasure drive" as a concept for a relaxing weekend adventure. Trains might have been an alternative to the terrors of New England driving, except at that time trains in the northeast were about at the lowest ebb in their long history so train travel was pretty miserable too. So for the balance of 1969 and 1970, there was very little train travel, or travel of any kind, for that matter. First, I had to get used to my new students and they had to get used to me.

Shades of past glory entering Providence.

It was about at this time that I made a c h a n c e discovery that w o u l d influence my travel for the rest of my professional

78

life, especially my rail travel. I had gone into biology and teaching because I had loved both since I was a pre-teen. The pay wasn't that good, compared to industry or government but if you worked on stuff that was interesting to anybody but a specialist, I found out that *people would pay you to come talk to them!* I worked on how and why birds fly in organized groups, and everybody has seen geese flying in V's and wondered why they do it. So I would go to professional meetings, and get invitations to talk in Emporia, Kansas, or Fayetteville, Arkansas, or wherever. Invitations to go to Paris were, alas, less frequent, but still, you have to start someplace–.

The *Canadian* in the Rockies.

The first record I found of a transcontinental trip I made after coming to Rhode Island was in September of 1970, a year after my arrival. I took the Canadian Pacific's *Canadian* out to Seattle via Vancouver, B.C. for some reason (not that you really need a *reason* to go to Seattle). I suspect that I went out to meet with my old post-doc adviser, who I still was working with. Even though the railroad it belongs to has had its ups and downs (by 1970, the Canadian Pacific had changed to "CP Rail," a branding triumph if ever there was one), the train itself has always been a first class operation, at least during the 30 years that I was a rider. When you are on a train for four days, which you will be if you go from

Montreal to Vancouver, the dining car becomes a focal point of your trip. Pantry space is limited on a train, so on a long journey the kitchen has to stock up along the way, which allows it to take advantage of local provender. However, with concepts developed by the airline catering industry, there is typically less "cooking" and more "heating" on dining cars these days, except on luxury operations like

Chef takes a break on the *Canadien*.

the contemporary *Rocky Mountaineer*.

The following year, 1971, I made another Seattle trip, this time on the Burlington Northern. The purpose of this trip was to go to the annual meeting of the American Ornithologist's Union. By this time, I had graduate students at Rhode Island, and two of them, Skip Pomeroy and Dave Preble, drove cross-country in a VW Bug to meet me, camping along the way. My grad students of the day were as crazy as I was. They decided to come back to Rhode Island essentially non-stop. This may have been inspired by the "Cannonball Baker Sea-To-Shining-Sea Memorial Trophy Dash" transcontinental race sponsored by *Car and Driver* magazine in early 1971. I recall that Skip and Dave made it in a little more than 3 days. They were very tired afterwards.

Amtrak was formed in 1970 but didn't start running the nation's passenger trains until May 1971. The name "Amtrak" was coined by the design consultation firm of Lippincott and Margulies which in 1948 had contributed to the design of Preston Tucker's rather, ah, unusual automobile known incorrectly as the "Tucker Torpedo." The Margulies nickname for it was the "Tin Goose." It was, alas, not a success, which was perhaps not a good omen for the firm's later work on Amtrak. The original name for the National Railroad Passenger Corporation was "Railpax" which suggested either a "pact" (among all the competing railroads) to form a semi-nationalized passenger rail system, or "peace" (among all the competing railroads). Either way, there was no suggestion of America in the name, so L & M, in a stroke of brilliance came up with "Am-Track," and decided that the color scheme for America's railroad system should be—Red, White, and Blue!! I'm stretching my memory, but my recollection is that they received about $100,000 for this creative effort in 1970 dollars.

The Amtrak logo and color scheme didn't start to be used until 1972, so existing trains before that still had a "rainbow" effect. When I took the *Empire Builder* out of Chicago, instead of being the beautiful, integrated color scheme of pre-BN days, it was a hodge-podge of the predecessor railroads' colors and equipment The *Empire Builder* was one of the few trains that still used full-length dome cars. These were beloved of passengers, but an operational and fiscal nightmare for the railroads that operated them.

Empire Builder Great Dome car.

In 1971, railroads were still using cabooses on freight trains and semaphores in their signal systems. Before we became litigation happy as a nation, train crews were still happy to allow rail photographers

Meet in Montana.

to open the last door on a passenger train to get pictures of the receding track without panes of scratchy glass intervening between the camera and the scene. The dining cars on western trains were still first rate. There remained roses in the bud vases, and the water pitchers were silver rather than stainless.

Back east however, after the first traumatizing trip to Concord up in Massachusetts, I stayed pretty close to home base, which now was Kingston, Rhode Island. There was little of rail interest locally that immediately caught one's attention. There was a little shortline railroad, the Narragansett Pier, which ran from the New Haven station at Kingston to the seaside town of Narragansett, but its single-car freight trains ran about as often as Halley's Comet reappeared. The typical mainline passenger train running (more typically, limping) through Kingston was one or two clapped out GM E-unit diesels that were sometimes still painted in Pennsylvania Railroad livery, and a motley assortment of passenger cars, which might span three generations of ancestry.

Turbo Train at Kingston.

Breaking the monotony was the twice daily appearance of the *Turbo Train,* so-called because it used gas turbine rather than diesel engines. This was a distant ancestor of the Acela trains today–at least in concept. The Shoreline Route between Boston and New York has many curves because it follows the coast line. This makes it very scenic but not conducive to high speeds because trains generally have to slow for curves. The Spaniards developed a new type of suspension to address this issue for their early attempts at high speed trains in the '50s. Essentially, the body of the train hangs from a pivot at the top of the cars, allowing the carbody to swing out, or tilt, as it enters the curve, much as an airplane banks. The *Turbo Train* was the first American train to use this design.

The two American turbo trains were made by United Aircraft in Connecticut. They followed airplane rather than train construction, in that instead of having a heavy frame atop which rested a lightweight body, they had a "monocoque" construction. The light weight of the body meant that when the train entered a tight curve, the car body would swing out rapidly. Because it didn't have lateral shock absorbers, after the curve the body would begin to swing back and forth, providing a nice simulation of the Block Island ferry in a quartering Nor'easter in February. I don't remember that the term "vomit comet" was used at the time, but old-timers invariably recall it in those terms. The modern Acela trains also have a tilting suspension but the concept has improved so much that you're not even aware of the tilt.

My horizons began to slowly expand. There was no real "campus community" around the URI campus, but there was one in Providence surrounding Brown University. There one could find used book stores, funky clothing emporia, and coffee houses. There were also restaurants in Providence, establishments that were in short supply in rural southern Rhode Island.

I can't begin to express how dismal and depressing Providence was at the beginning of the '70s. I grew up in the Italian district of San Francisco, North Beach. It was lively, colorful, noisy, and safe. Little mom-and-pop Italian restaurants were everywhere. You couldn't walk more than two blocks without getting hungry again, no matter when you last ate because the wonderful smells permeated everything. The fact that the Ghirardelli chocolate factory was about 10 blocks from where I lived, and on Tuesdays roasted cocoa beans didn't hurt, either.

Providence's Italian neighborhood was Federal Hill, or colloquially "The Hill." I will not name the place, but its most well known restaurant at the time had that status because a couple of mob guys got whacked in one of the booths, and they left the bullet holes for the tourists. They generally featured two kinds of wine, red and white, and both were served "ice-cold" just like the beers. Walking around the Hill was just creepy, and non-natives didn't linger.

Nevertheless, as it now appeared that I was going to be in Rhode Island

Waiting for the Grim Reaper.

for a while I decided to do a little rail exploration and found myself in the Providence engine yards of the Penn Central. I took a picture of a couple of at-death's-door Penn Central Alco RS locomotives that expressed the depressing reality of railroading in Rhode Island at the time. The turntable and roundhouse had an after-the-apocalypse-is-over quality

Kingston and Providence having pretty much exhausted their supply of rail interest in a short period I started widening my travel circle a bit, mostly in the direction of New York. The Shoreline Route between Boston and New Haven was not electrified until 2000, so before that trains were pulled by diesel locomotives from Boston to New Haven. There, the diesel engine(s) were pulled off, and electric engines slipped on for the rest of the journey to Washington, DC via New York City. Twenty minutes were usually allowed for this maneuver, but crews could do it in ten if they were late and humped their butts. While the change was taking place, passengers could get off and take a smoke break or in my case, take pictures.

The GG-1.

To the west of the New Haven station platforms, there was a small engine yard, and in the early '70s, one could occasionally find one of the legendary Pennsylvania Railroad GG-1 electric locomotives. The GG-1 is on almost all American railfan's Favorite Locomotive list, because it practically defines the '30s streamlined age. It was designed and built when the Pennsylvania Railroad called itself the Standard Railroad of the World, and they meant it.

The GG-1 was made to haul 18 car trains at 100 mph between New York Penn Station and Washington. The ubiquitous Art Deco industrial designer Raymond Loewy had a hand in the finishing touches of the design of the GG-1's. They had started their career with the Pennsy, and when that railroad was homologated with the New York Central to form the Penn Central the GG-1s were repainted black with the

PC's entwined worms logo. The PC went belly up almost as soon as it was formed, and Amtrak picked up 50 GG-1's for its northeast corridor service. When I saw them in New Haven in the early-mid 70s, they were

GG-1 and E unit at New Haven yard.

pretty well clapped out, like the survivors of the PC diesel fleet.

New Haven and Bridgeport were actually pretty interesting places for railfans in the mid '70s. You could see both electric and diesel locomotives, and weird stuff that Amtrak had picked up, usually at bargain prices, from its ancestors. One of the stranger pieces of equipment was something called the *Roger Williams*, named after the founder of Rhode Island. It was kind of a cross between a streetcar and a diesel locomotive. Originally called "RDC's" or rail diesel cars, these were self-propelled passenger cars that were used to replace conventional trains on low patronage routes, usually as a single car. In 1956, the New Haven ordered up a whole train of six RDC's. The two units on the end were equipped with engine cabs. In short order the train was split up, and when I saw it at Bridgeport, it was being operated as a two-car train. As a sign of the times, the cab windows of the *Roger Williams* were covered with heavy steel grates. This is because city kids had discovered an amusing new sport. They would stand on an overpass that crossed the tracks, and as soon as the engine was within 25 feet or so of the bridge, they'd drop a concrete block tied to the end of rope over the bridge rail, and see if they could smash the cab windshield. After a couple of engineers were knocked out, the screens were introduced. Bullet-proof glass has now replaced the grills.

Roger Williams at New Haven.

In the mid-'70s Amtrak started testing new locomotives to replace the now-senile GG-1's. One of their more bizarre choices was the General Electric E-60. The E-60 was originally designed to haul long trains full of coal in Arizona, and it had the design sensibilities that you might expect for such a task. It looked like a slightly melted, gigantic cube of butter sitting on 12 wheels. Other than a slight tendency to derail at speed, and a porcine weight (for a passenger train electric engine) of 387,000 pounds they gave reasonably satisfactory service, but they had a short service life, in some cases, only 10 years .

In train photography, a lot of luck is involved. One day in New Haven, probably around 1976, I caught an E-60, an RDC, and a brand new F40PH (which was to become Amtrak's flagship diesel engine for the next 25 years) in the engine staging yard. All were in spanking new paint jobs, and lined up as if they were posing. I got the slide back from processing, and when I looked at it closely, I saw something I had missed when I took the picture. In the right background behind the shiny new engines was a poor, old, decrepit Penn Central E-8 passenger locomotive, its salad days in the '50s long over, now patiently awaiting the scrapper's torch.

Sic transit gloria mundi.

Chapter 7
Here, There, and Everywhere

By 1973, I had tenure at URI, a laboratory with grad and undergrad students underfoot everywhere, and I was starting to dabble in real estate. My mother was still having health problems back in San Francisco, so I had to go back and check up on her once or twice a year. I usually took the train, but by now, I'd gotten over the screaming heebie-jeebies about flying, which was a good thing, because passenger trains were disappearing like groupies around last year's boy band.

However, by '73-'74, Amtrak was *beginning* to get its act together. Strangely, many of its early national-level executives were drawn from the airline industry, and they seemed to have the mindset that people weren't riding trains because they didn't look like airplanes. So the first generation of single-level cars that Amtrak ordered in the '70s looked like–airplanes. They were called "Amfleet" cars. They had little tiny windows, undoubtedly to protect passengers from the low air pressure around Denver. They were also tubular in cross section, like an airliner, but they were made of corrugated steel, so they kind of looked like the fuselage of, say, a '30s Ford Tri-Motor plane.

Someone in their "branding" group decided that everything on board the train had to be prefaced by "Am-." So we had Amcafe cars, Amcoach cars, and Amlounge cars. So you could get a cup of Amcoffee in the Amcafe, and then go get an Ammartini to kill the taste of the Amcoffee. There were new conductor's uniforms that looked like air crew uniforms. If there was any way they could have put little stubby wings on the coaches, they probably would have.

This was ironic and hilarious. In 1967, Pacific Air Lines, a regional carrier on the west coast hired radio comedian and ad man Stan Freberg to develop an ad campaign to forthrightly deal with passengers' fear of flying, which no airline had ever mentioned before. Stewardesses handed out "survival kits" containing rabbits' feet and security blankets. They also were instructed to say upon landing, "We made it! How about that?" At a press conference, Freberg outlined plans to paint smokestacks and drive wheels on their 727s, and have some sort of projection device so that when the passengers looked out the window, they'd see telephone poles going by.

The campaign was understandably very short lived, and a couple of PAL's execs who had been responsible for hiring Freberg lost their jobs afterwards. Although the campaign is legendary in advertising circles as one of the worst ad campaigns ever, it was not as bizarre or irrational as it looks from this distance. There had been 5 fatal accidents involving Boeing 727's in 1965 and 1966, and PAL had just ordered a half dozen 727's that were to be put in service in 1967. Since they were introduced in 1963, 6% of all the 727's built have crashed. Whether Freberg's approach would have been effective or not certainly could be argued, but there was no doubt that the flying public was VERY nervous about flying in the mid-'60s, as well they should have been. There may have been another issue, however. Freberg was an enthusiastic train rider, and when I was in the Davis Railroad Club and we were planning our anti-SP campaigns, we corresponded with Freberg, and he had some good suggestions. So I've always had a sneaking feeling that Freberg, who was as eccentric as they come, may have planned the campaign deliberately to sink the airline. Just a thought.

No longer having a railroad pass as in the days of my youth, when I traveled cross-country I had my choice of routes. Because it was most direct route, I usually took the old SP-UP Overland Route; Denver-Cheyenne-Ogden-SF. The Denver and Rio Grande Western was one of the few passenger railroads that didn't join Amtrak in 1970, but they still ran their section of the old *California Zephyr* between Denver and Salt Lake City. They renamed it the *Rio Grande Zephyr*. There's not a generally accepted definitive reason why the Rio Grande took this step; the two main reasons offered were that it would have been cheaper for them to continue to run their own train, rather than pony up the large "admission fee" required to pass on their passenger trains to Amtrak, and more obscurely (and less convincingly to me), they were concerned that Amtrak operations would somehow interfere with their freight operations over their single track.

One of those transcon trips in '73 suggests the changes that were taking place. Amtrak had absorbed many of the passenger diesel engines from the "donor" railroads, but had not yet repainted them in Amtrak colors. As a result, you could see engines from three different primary railroads

E "variety pack" in Denver.

at the head end of your train. This caused endless operational problems for Amtrak, because although all locomotives of a single type, say an E-8, might have been identical when they left the factory, the individual railroads customized them for their own operating practices. So an SP engineer today might have an SP E-8, but tomorrow a UP version, and they wouldn't handle the same, or operate the same. On the other hand, railroads that took pride in their operation, like UP, kept their freight service equipment in perfect shape.

Union Pacific "big hook."

Denver was a major junction point for railroads beginning a Rockies crossing, and it also was a center for rich railfans who owned their own railroad equipment. One such was a man named Glenn Monhart, a wealthy young shortline railroad owner from Wisconsin, who operated his own roundhouse, and owned a beautifully restored early diesel engine painted in Seaboard Coast Line livery, and an entire train of *Nebraska Zephyr* cars. Much to the surprise of many people, there are still privately owned, operating railroad cars in the US (about 150 as of today), and Amtrak has an 11 page contract that private car owners sign to have their cars hauled by Amtrak. The cost to own one is much less than owning a small jet, and the operating costs are in the same ballpark. Not want to bother with ownership? You can charter one for $2-3,000 a day, and carry 12 of your friends. To carry that many passengers on a private jet from Boston to DC, would cost you $10,000. *Anybody* with a few bucks in his/her pocket can charter a (yawn) jet, but only a (rich) person of style and distinction would have the good taste to arrive in town by private railroad car.

Privately owned early E-unit at Denver.

One of the problems with writing a memoir like this is that memory is imperfect. I found some pictures that I took of the Southern Railroad's *Southern Crescent* train stopped at Birmingham, Alabama in 1974. I cannot for the life of me remember WHY I was on the *Crescent*, but two possibilities come to mind. I could have been going to the West Coast the long way. The VERY long way, recreating my trip home in disgrace after I left Rennselaer Polytechnic in New York. Unlikely. Or, I could have been going to scientific meetings that I know were held in Norman, Oklahoma. Equally unlikely, because I would have had to go from Birmingham to New Orleans to Houston, and then up to OK-city, and then a bus. So, I'm going to call it still a mystery.

Southern Crescent, somewhere in the deep South.

Not a mystery is the significance of the *Southern Crescent* to Amtrak history. At the formation of Amtrak, four passenger-carrying railroads did not join. Two were very small, one was the Rio Grande, and the other was the Southern. Whereas there is still some controversy about why the Rio Grande didn't join, there is no controversy about the Southern's reluctance. At the time, the Southern was headed by a truly remarkable man named W. Graham Claytor, a fourth-generation railroad man whose great-great-grandfather established the ancestor of the Southern Railroad in 1827.

Claytor was a Harvard *summa cum laude*, a law clerk to Supreme Court Justice Learned Hand, a WWII naval hero, and took over the presidency of the Southern in 1967. He was an "operating" president, and preferred finding out how things were going by being in the cab of an engine, than by getting memos. He was enormously proud of the Southern's passenger trains, and was convinced that because Amtrak was started with such short funding that if they took over the Southern's passenger fleet, it would quickly be run into the ground. Claytor retired from the presidency of the Southern in 1977, and the line ran the *Crescent* independently until 1979, when the capital costs of replacement equipment for the train would have been prohibitive, and reluctantly, the *Crescent* was turned over to Amtrak. Ironically, in 1982 Claytor was asked to come out of retirement to run Amtrak, which he did until 1993.

By 1976, my mother was starting to show the signs of age out in San Francisco, and I knew that she wouldn't be able to live indefinitely in the apartment she kept after my Dad died in 1967. She'd always wanted to go to Europe, but never had the opportunity. At the time I was doing pretty well financially, so I decided to take her on a trip–a first class trip–to Europe. Such a trip would be beyond my wildest imaginings today, but at the time it was do-able.

Naturally, we *had* to go over by ship, and I thought it would be sort of delicious to see how the other side lived on the same ship I'd taken in 1969, the *QE2*. As I quickly discovered, the other side lived very well, indeed.

There had been some changes over six years. Although designed as a three-class ship (first, cabin, and tourist) like the older liners, the distinctions had become fuzzy, and the difference between first and tourist class was really in the restaurant to which you were assigned, and the public rooms to which you had access. However, unlike on the *Titanic* where there was rigid physical separation between the classes–after all, Mrs. VanderRocks wouldn't want to come within smelling distance of a tourist passenger-by the time of *QE2*, the classes were separated merely by a series of unlocked, unmarked doors. A sufficiently brazen tourist class person who had a nice, well fitting suit could pass unnoticed into the higher class's bars, dance floors, etc., although he couldn't cadge a first class meal, because folks had assigned table seats. Trespassing worked both ways. The affluent could rather easily sneak into tourist class. Why would a rich dude in first *want* to go to tourist? Well, if he were a rich *young* dude, the average age of the single female travelers in tourist was about 25 years younger than the dowagers traveling in his own class, and the parties were a lot more fun. It was the '70s, after all.

The cabaret of the *QE 2*.

Mom took to it like the proverbial duck to water. She loved to go to the cabaret and dance the night away. She was 68, but still could do a mean jitterbug. She was getting a little hard of hearing, and you had to repeat things, but the pace of shipboard life seemed to suit her. The First Class dining room had a relaxed atmosphere, and it really did practice Burger

King's recently introduced slogan, "Have it your way!" Didn't see what you want on the menu? Tell the Maitre d' and give him 15 extra minutes, and it would be yours.

We landed in France at Le Havre, where there was a wonderful boat train terminal. There was some time before the train left for Paris, so I left Mom in the compartment and wandered around the platform. Up near the engine I saw something that brought on a twinge of nostalgia. A father and his budding railfan son were chatting up the engineer at the head end of the train .

"À quelle vitesse ça va, monsieur?"

We stayed in Paris for a couple of days, and had dinner at the legendary Lucas Carton, alas now gone to the great banquet hall in the sky. Our final destination would be Switzerland. From Paris, we took a TEE. The French TEE cars at the time were clad on the exterior with stainless steel like the

Amfleet cars, but they somehow looked elegant and sophisticated, instead of like Greyhound buses.

On the way out of Paris as we were passing through a suburban yard, I snapped a picture of a locomotive that I later found out belonged to a very famous class of engine-the SNCF (French National Railways) 7100 series.

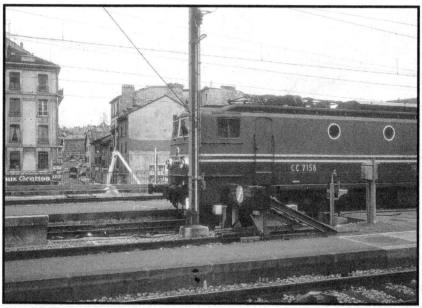

World's fastest locomotive (at the time).

The 7100's were electric locomotives that had been built in the mid '50s to haul heavy passenger trains. In 1955, CC 7107 broke the world rail speed record by a wide margin, topping 200 mph for the first time. This record was held for over *50 years*! It is difficult to see how this was done. The engine could only draw 4,680 horsepower, and had virtually no streamlining.

We had lunch on the TEE *en route* to Geneva. In Europe, "waiter" was considered to be a skilled profession, and good waiters were paid well and respected in the community. Our waiter was a young Italian man–I'll not

99

claim a memory so good that I remember his name, but we'll call him Sergio. He flattered my mother outrageously, and I was a bit worried that she'd get off the train with him when we arrived, but she came to her senses.

Sergio charms Mom on the TEE.

The TEE trains made crossing borders very simple, and it seemed like no time before we were in Switzerland. To a railfan, one of the first things that strikes you about the Swiss railroad system is that everything is neat, tidy, and shiny. It really is true that you can set your watch by the departure of a Swiss train (unless it is scheduled to leave exactly on the hour. The second hands on Swiss railway station clocks pause at 58.5 seconds, then jump to the 00:00:00 position. So you could be as much as a second and a half off).

Once we left Lucerne, we made a loop through Interlaken, and then down to Visp. Along the way, we passed a spot well known to Sherlock Holmes fans, the Reichenbach Falls. The Falls is where Holmes allegedly met his death at the hands of Professor Moriarity. Ah, but we know the truth about that story, don't we?

I had wanted to make the high point of the trip an excursion to Zermatt, so Mom could see the Matterhorn. This meant taking the Zermatt Bahn, and then the Gornergrat Bahn cog railways, as I had done several times before. But I made a miscalculation.

Mom had always been pretty fearless. She had been born in North Korea, where my grandfather was a mining engineer at the great Taracol gold mine. The mine was 50 miles by muleback from the nearest railhead. As a teenager in Auburn, she had ridden horseback with her friends on the Rubicon trail to Hell Hole on the American River. As a nurse in San Francisco during the Roaring Twenties, she was one of the few staffers that didn't mind treating gangsters brought to the hospital after shootouts.

The Reichenbach Falls.

But the years had taken their toll. The Zermatt Bahn train travels along a very narrow ledge between a wall on one side, and a cliff on the other. It quickly developed that she *really didn't like* sitting on the side of the car where you looked down into the apparently bottomless pit of the canyon. So, as the train shifted from one side of the canyon to the other over bridges, she'd move from side to side of the car (it wasn't crowded, fortunately).

When we arrived at Zermatt, I got a couple of beers into her, and I must say, she was a trooper. When the Gornergrat train started pointing skyward, there wasn't a whimper out of her. In the interest of accuracy, I have to say that in the one picture I have of her standing on the viewing platform at Gornergrat, she has a rather frozen smile.

Zermatt really marked the end of the trip. We went back to Paris, and as part of the deal with first class fares on the *QE2* we got to return to New York first class on a British Airways 747. That was good news and bad news. The good news was that it was wonderful. The bad news was that it spoiled me for riding air coach, and coach air travel has now descended into the same bottomless canyon that was at the base of the Zermatt Bahn tracks. I can't believe that in the late '60s, I *complained* about the small size of the *filet mignon* steak they gave you in air coach, and the fact that the free bottle of wine was from California.

I sent Mom back to her apartment in California. Later events would show that the timing of the trip was perfect. In '77, it became painfully apparent that she was no longer capable of taking care of herself independently, and I had to put her in an assisted care facility. However, whenever I went out to visit her in San Francisco, all I had to do was mention "Zermatt" and her face lit up. Sometimes, you get it right.

Chapter 8

Into the '80s, or, Not Everybody Had a Mullet

The decade of the seventies was a time of transition for the United States. We moved from the "swingin' sixties" to "greed is good" in about a dozen years. Big bands had disappeared, rock was evolving, and while we were waiting to see where it would go, we had disco (embarrassing personal confession; I *liked* disco. It was about the last pop music form where you actually had to know how to dance with prescribed steps, rather than just twerk your partner. I was pretty good at swing and jitterbug, so I could dance like John Travolta, except badly). Off the dance floor, Americans had to deal with some brand new situations–.

In January of 1980, I had been invited to give a lecture at the University of Cambridge. After the lecture, I had dinner at High Table with the begowned Dons of the college. Pretty snooty bunch. With the port after dinner, the conversation turned to the Iran hostage situation, which was in its second month. I remarked to the distinguished scholar sitting next to me that as an American, it was a strange and humiliating situation for America, the most powerful country in the world, to be powerless in the face of a tinpot religious fanatic. "But dear boy," he said in unctuous, smarmy fashion. "You aren't the most powerful country in the world any more!"

Wow.

Just as the country (and the world) was changing at a breathtaking clip, so was my own professional and personal life. My career was really starting to take off, which involved a lot of travel, and I now was "commuting" between Rhode Island, and Grosse Point, Michigan, where my son and his mother then lived. Sometimes I flew but I usually took the *Lake Shore Limited*. Basically only masochists or railfans took the *Lake Shore* from Rhode Island to Detroit or return at the time. Here's why.

The first problem was that the train didn't actually go to Detroit. It went to Toledo, Ohio, and you then took a bus to Detroit. So you had to change at Toledo. Now I'm sure Toledo is a lovely city, but coming from the east, the *Lake Shore* arrived in Toledo at 5:55 AM, not a time when cities or people look their best. The bus then left a half hour later for the hour ride to Detroit. But wait! It gets better. Going in the other direction, the bus left Detroit at 9:00 PM, for a 10:05 PM arrival in Toledo. Then, you only had a five-and-a-half hour wait in the Toledo station until the train was scheduled to leave at a little after 3 AM. Have trouble getting to sleep if you only have five-and-a-half hours on a bench? Not to worry! The train's on time record was 65%, so you might have had MUCH longer to snooze. The train's semi-official nickname was "Late-for-sure Limited."

When I first started making this run in the late '70s, Amtrak was still using the old Michigan Central train station in Detroit, near the original Tiger Stadium. At one time this was one of the most impressive stations in the country, but the building had been allowed to fall into ruin and there was a definite post-apocalyptic vibe about it when you showed up at night for your bus. It had an urban "Night of the Living Dead" feeling, and was pretty much a home for the homeless--their shadowy figures added a zombie tone to the experience.

The western part of the run was for the masochists, but the eastern part was really pretty good for railfans. Westward bound out of Rhode Island, you could start in either of two ways; up to Boston for the New England section of the *Lake Shore*, or down to New York for the New York section. The New York and Boston sections were combined at Albany into a single train for the run west. Both runs were best in summer to early fall, when there is still daylight to at least 8 PM.

The New England section runs from Boston to Springfield, and then starts heading through the Berkshire mountains. These would not be "Mountains" to a Coloradan, but they're impressive in their own right, and in the fall they're sensational. The New York section follows the old New York Central "water level" route up the east bank of the Hudson River. The best side to sit on is the west side of the train–the views are stunning, almost like going up the Rhine.

The two sections meet across the river from Albany at a place called Rensselaer. Yes, Rensselaer, just like the Rensselaer Polytechnic Institute, which is only a few miles away. I always made sure I was well inoculated with strong waters before the train pulled in for its half hour wait. I was afraid some of the bad ju-ju from RPI might still be lingering in the air, and I'd find my IQ dropping by 20 points or so if I got off the train for a stretch.

The train has had its ups and downs over the years, but I have to give Amtrak credit for at least sometimes trying to take advantage of the beauty of the eastern part of the run and if you traveled in the sleeping car, making you feel that it was at least semi-"first-class." For a while, you got a little package of toiletries, like you do in air Business Class, and there was a very nice printed route guide. Alas, all gone to train Heaven now.

In the late '70s, academia was awash with money (in many places), and if one played one's cards right, this availability could translate into travel. In 1979, I got invited to address the Japan Ornithological Society in Tokyo in early 1980 on their dime. Japan's economy was doing well, but hadn't entered the bubble period of the '80s. Pan American Airways was still flying, and I discovered that for less than the price of a round trip Boston-Tokyo, I could buy a round-the-world ticket. This service had just started, and I believe you had to complete your trip in 80 days ("Around the World in Eighty Days," he, he). I think you could make at least a dozen stops. I figured that in at least some of the places, I'd get to ride trains. The whole trip took about 3 weeks.

Having my foot in the door, as it were, in Tokyo, I managed to kill many birds with one stone (we ornithologists don't really like this old saying). I told my counterparts at the University of Hong Kong that I was going to be in their neck of the woods after I finished in Tokyo, and if they'd be willing to put me up, I'd be happy to give them a talk, too. One of my teaching assistant's families lived in Hong Kong, so I made arrangements to give them news of their honorable son. Unknown to me at the time, this little detour later turned out to have huge dividends, because another of my former students was in the Peace Corps out in the *bundocks* on the Island of Mindanao in the Philippines, so I made arrangements to go from Hong Kong to Manila and then down to Mindanao to gave another talk at Xavier University in Cagayan de Oro City where she was stationed. This eventually led to a year in Asia a year or so later.

From Mindanao, I was scheduled to go back to Manila, and thence to New Delhi, with a side trip to Kathmandu in Nepal, so I could see Mount Everest. Back to India, then a refueling stop in Dubai, and then London. From there, I bopped up to Cambridge, and pulled the same deal with guest lectures as I did in Hong Kong. Then it was back to my drab existence in Kingston.

As I look back at the pictures of this trip, I'm reminded of how much travel, especially "budget" travel has changed since then. Being a "flight attendant" today carries no cachet, but Pan Am stewardesses all had to have college degrees when such degrees were far more unusual than they are today. They also had to be fluent in *at least* one other language besides English. I won't say coach passengers were treated royally, but we were treated very well, the planes weren't sardine cans with wings, and the food was actually pretty good.

The first leg of the trip was my first experience with a Boeing 747, and then as now, I'm still awestruck at this engineering achievement. The first time you see one up close, you invariably say, "There is no possible way this thing can get off the ground without its wings snapping off." But then it does, and they don't.

Late-lamented Pan American Airways Boeing 747SP long-range transoceanic airliner in Hawaii. Next stop; Guam.

Aircraft now can make the west-coast/Japan hop nonstop, but then there were refueling stops in Hawaii and/or Guam. I never left the airport in Hawaii, but I figured Guam might be worth an overnight stop, and it was–sort of. There were two main industries in Guam at the time, American defense bases, and shopping malls for Japanese shoppers. Sales taxes on luxury goods in Japan were so high that it was worthwhile for Japanese entrepreneurs to charter airplanes to bring Japanese shoppers to Guam, where there were no taxes. The irony of the difference between the invasion of Guam by Japanese soldiers in the '40s, and affluent Japanese shoppers in the '80s did not escape me.

Guam was of enormous interest to students of WWII, due to the fierce battles that took place in 1941 and 1945, but in the '80s there was little to be seen by the casual visitor. Similarly, Guam provides a textbook case for the enormous ecological destruction caused by invasive species. The mildly venomous brown tree snake was introduced to Guam shortly after

WWII, found it to its liking, and immediately began reproducing uncontrollably, reaching a density of 100 snakes per acre all over the island. One of their favorite kinds of food is–you guessed it– endangered species of birds, of which Guam had a number. Unfortunately, my casual and brief visit didn't really allow real time for exploration and my take-away conclusion was that Guam was boring.

Japan was completely different. I was picked up at the airport by my Japanese host, which was a good thing, because Japan was the first place I had ever visited that was *really different* from home. Growing up in San Francisco, I had some exposure to Japanese culture, but as I quickly discovered, there is the Japanese culture of Zen, exquisite design, superb craftsmanship, and art characterized by simplicity of line, and then there is the OTHER Japanese culture of bizarre Japlish ("No Smorking in Building"), garish neon lights that rival the sun in intensity, and terminal cuteness (Hello Kitty). As there was virtually no English visible in the terminal (this situation has changed), I was more than glad to have someone meet me.

I didn't get a chance to do much independent sightseeing as my hosts quite reasonably figured that I would get lost and not show up for my talk, but I did discover something. Those people were SERIOUS about food. I was advised that one of the best tempura restaurants in Tokyo was within easy walking distance of my hotel. My second night in the city I strolled over, and discovered a tiny hole-in-the-wall place, with a long counter. I sat down, the chef came over, smiled, and asked me what seemed to be a question. In retrospect, I think he was asking me if I wanted the daily special, which was tuna anus, with a special marinated caterpillar sauce. I nodded my head vigorously and smiled broadly. He then set to work deep-frying a single battered piece of whatever it was and then placed it on my plate. When I finished, he fried up the next piece, and this procedure was repeated for the whole meal. I believe the idea was that each morsel had to be served at EXACTLY the correct temperature. Whether it was really tuna anus or not, it was delicious, and I had never tasted anything remotely like it.

My hosts had arranged my hotel, and they had asked me if I wanted a western-style room or a Japanese room. Naturally, I selected the Japanese-style, and it was fine once I figured out how to use the Japanese-style squat toilet. Next day, I had a choice between a Western or Japanese breakfast. I chose the latter. The waiter seemed startled to see me and asked something in Japanese. I nodded enthusiastically. He seemed surprised, but soon brought back a bowl of steaming noodles in some kind of broth. I picked up a big wad of noodles with my chopsticks, popped them in my mouth, and GAAAHHHH!! I had never tasted anything so vile in my life. The noodles were also sticky, so I couldn't just swallow them, and of course, I couldn't spit them out. They stuck to my teeth, so I could enjoy the horrible rotting corpse taste for several minutes. I later found out that a big part of *real* Asian cooking involved using fermented fish sauce. You spread fresh fish out on a rack, wait til it rots and decomposes, then catch the juice. Yum! Over the course of the years, I actually discovered that I liked the stuff, but it comes in several strengths, and the waiter was probably asking me if I wanted what would be the Japanese equivalent of Texas five star molten hell chili. The typical American hibachi joint bears no resemblance to actual Japanese cooking.

My talk went well and I indicated to my hosts that I'd like to see one of their fast *hikari* trains. "Shinkansen" is the name usually attached to these trains in the west, but that word actually refers to the rail line. They were a bit puzzled at the strange desires of their American guest, but were more than happy to take me to Tokyo station and get me on the platform without a ticket.

It was overwhelming. The *crowds*. Never seen anything like it, even in Manhattan. There were train boards everywhere, where you could see which train went where, on what track, and at what time. That is, you could see those things if you read Japanese; otherwise it was just numbers. With a little help from my hosts, I figured out that they were running these fast, main line trains on *seven minute headings* during rush hour. There were 25 *hikari* non-stop trains a day between Tokyo and Kyoto, and the same number of locals.

Hikari pulling into station.

The *hikaris* hold about 1,500 passengers, and they could load and unload the whole train in about 2 minutes. I later found out how they did it. On the incoming train, they make an announcement of arrival about 90 seconds before. Everybody who's getting off and is on an aisle seat stands up, gets their bags, and stands in the aisle facing the front door. People in the window seats get ready to move.

On the platform, waiting for the incoming, everybody has a ticket with their car number printed on it. They find a line painted on the platform, parallel to the track, with their car number on it and at the end, a little "hook" facing the tracks. Everybody lines up on the line facing the hook. When the train comes into the station, the engineer stops the train about plus or minus two *inches* so that the hook for a particular car number is directly opposite the back door of the car. The train stops, all doors open, and the people in the aisle trot out the front door. As the end of the line passes the last people who had window seats in the back of the car, they start joining the line from the back. As soon as the there is room at the very end of the line, the passengers waiting to board start to file in from the back.

My first reaction to seeing this was amazement. It was so *efficient!* Could it work in America? Naaah, we're cowboys. We hate lines, unless they're for tickets for a rock show. My second reaction was embarrassment. We *whipped* these folks in World War II, and they had this incredible system, but we had the *Lakeshore Limited.* They had these gorgeous ultra fast trains and we had Amfleet cars.

I calmed down a bit when I recalled that the Japanese rail system was built, brand-new-from-scratch after World War II when the country was essentially flattened to the ground, whereas we had an old, tired infrastructure still in place. Plus, America had largely *paid* for the beautiful Japanese rail system after the war as a very successful strategy of turning enemies into customers. It seemed to have worked with a vengeance.

Then it was off to Hong Kong. This staggeringly beautiful city was built on hills, like San Francisco so I felt sort-of like home. They still had an extensive and well-used streetcar system, in addition to the usual suburban train network that most cities of the day had. The streetcars were odd because they were double-deckers, like the buses in London

I had a dual mission. First, to give a talk at the University of Hong Kong, and second to act as a messenger and send greetings and news to the family of my teaching assistant Dennis. Dennis' cousin Paul picked me up at the airport, and I quickly discovered that a bizarre mistake had been made. I

Hong Kong double-deck tram.

was getting the full-on VIP treatment! I don't know what Dennis had told his family, but Paul had a schedule of meetings for me with high level leaders of Hong Kong's higher education and political communities, including the Chair of Hong Kong's Communist Party (Hong Kong even back then was setting up for the eventual transfer of government from the Brits to the mainland). I had no idea why I was meeting them, or what they expected me to talk about, but all my earlier training as a bullshit artist came into full play.

I had about one day to be a tourist so naturally I made a beeline to the Peak Tram funicular.A funicular is a kind of cable car, but instead of having a moving cable and cars that can attach or detatch like those in San Francisco, there is a single cable that passes around a pulley at the top of the hill. Attached to the ends of the cable are two passenger cars that act as counterweights for each other. If the funicular has but a single track, there is a passing track in the middle of the run. The Peak Tram climbs about 1,300 feet to the top of Victoria Peak, which has one of the world's great views.

The next couple of days are kind of lost in a fog. I gave my talk in the afternoon of the second day, but then Dennis' family had me scheduled for dinner meetings with the dignitaries I was supposed to meet. The reason I was in a fog was because I discovered what you drink at a high-end Chinese dinner. Cognac. Sometimes Scotch. Lots of it.

Hong Kong Peak Tram funicular.

The first night's dinner was at the newly opened "Jumbo Palace" floating restaurant. It was during this first banquet that I discovered *why* these folks wanted to talk to me. Hong Kong was in the process of moving away from the traditional format for university education of lecture-memorize notes-don't ask questions Asian approach to a more Western open kind of education, and they had no experience with this. I was developing a certain expertise and reputation in teaching college teachers how to teach using student participation, and it was THAT info that my assistant Dennis had passed on to Hong Kong. At this point, I started to feel comfortable about accepting these free meals that I would have to take out a second mortgage to buy if I paid myself. My hosts made out because they got a consultant without having to pay a fee and airfare.

Okay, might as well get it out of the way. At all my meals I ate the most politically incorrect foods you could imagine. Bird's nest soup. Shark fin soup. "Special beef." (I won't say what it was, but if you see it on a menu, don't order it). By this time, I knew that it was an inflexible rule of Asian etiquette not to refuse a gift. I'd never be able to go back to Hong Kong if I refused the *gei ji*, and the rooster probably didn't need them anymore anyway.

The second night's dinner was in a super-elegant restaurant in one of Hong Kong's skyscrapers. Unfortunately, I don't remember the name, but it looked like something in a James Bond movie. I'm sure I was less and less coherent as the night wore on, but after dinner my hosts insisted on taking me to a "night club." Well, it sort of looked like a night club. There were tables, a band, a dance floor, waiters, and menus. The waiter brought me a menu. Of course it was in Chinese, so I asked for a translation. The first entry was "Lihua (beautiful and elegant). 23. From Guilin Province. Speaks English and French. Lives only to please you. HK $2,000."

Oh, THAT kind of night club. How was I going to refuse? Fortunately, I really did have an early flight out next morning, and as it was already about 2 AM, I pleaded a need for rest. I was, after all, a scholar, and we need a lot of sleep. I brought the menu home with me, but I don't know where it is now. Sigh.

Next day, off to Manila, and a short hop down to the island of Mindanao to visit with my former student. I was only there for a day or so, but she arranged for me to meet with university officials and give a little talk. I was absolutely charmed by the place, even though I had never seen poverty even fractionally as bad. I thought it might be nice to come back some day and hunt for trains.

114

Back to Manila and the long hop to New Delhi. I wanted to see the Taj Mahal in Agra, and the main way to get there from Delhi was by train. Once I settled in, I went down to the train station, and discovered that the only trains I had time for were completely booked. I didn't fancy riding on the roof of the train, as I had seen passengers do in a number of pictures so I went back to the hotel and booked a car, driver and guide, for some ridiculously low sum of money.

The car, ominously, had a hole in the front bumper for a crank like my old MG. At the time, the only road between Delhi, a city of about 10 million population at the time, and Agra, a city of a million population, was a single two-lane highway.

As we got out of the city, the road passed over the railroad, and I asked the driver to stop so I could get a picture. My request was totally bizarre to the driver, but Americans, hey–. I was lucky enough to catch one of the still operating Indian steam engines. Pretty soon, we were out on the highway, and there I had a cultural insight that really changed my view of the world. The road was lined on both sides with little open-air shops and restaurants. Every once in a while you'd see a huge cart hauled by water buffalo, or a camel-driver leading four or five camels with packs. Not in Kansas any more.

Indian steam and diesel.

The most striking thing was that there were endless lines of people walking on either side of the road. I asked the guide about it.

"Swati." (I just made that up; I don't really remember his name).
Where are all these people going?"
He was puzzled. "Going, Sir?"
"Yes, where are they walking to?"
"Ah, nowhere, Sir. They can walk or they can sit. Those are their
choices."

This hit me between the eyes. I had been brought up with the American
middle-class vision of life. If you're smart, and work hard, you can rise
above any economic hardship. Horatio Alger. But for these Indian walkers,
it didn't matter how smart they were or how hard they worked; they were
always going to be walking along the Agra road. Right place-right time are
sometimes equal to or more important than brains or hard work. Unpleasant
truth, but it made me a lot less cocky about my admittedly good fortune to
date.

No more trains in India, but then a short hop up to Nepal, because I had
been fascinated by
Mount Everest ever
since I was a young
teenager. You
couldn't see
Everest from the
capital city.
However at the
airport, I found that
Royal Nepal
Airlines flew
sightseeing flights
around Everest in a

Royal Nepal Airlines puddlejumper.

116

clapped-out Hawker-Siddley HS-748 turboprop. I booked a flight for next day.

I had gotten a pilot's license in 1977, and this was a new airplane for me. Once we were airborne, I told the stewardess that I was a pilot, and would it be okay if I went up to the cockpit? She said sure, so I walked up and knocked on the cockpit door. Somebody said, "Come in," and I saw that the pilot and co-pilot were both reading newspapers while the plane was on autopilot. The view out the cockpit window was stunning. The pilot asked me if I'd ever flown a Hawker before. I replied in the negative, but with a tone of voice that suggested that I *had* flown 747's, F-16's, etc. He then asked me if I'd like to fly it for a while. Oh, no! I'd just *hate* it. So he got in the jump seat, and I flew the plane past Mount Everest. When I was a kid I had been *inflamed* by reading Sir Edmund Hillary's "Conquest of Everest" and the thought that I was now only about ten miles from the summit was almost too much to take.

Everest from the cockpit.

The rest of the trip was anticlimactic. Back to Delhi, with a continuation to London via Dubai. Once in London, I visited the Sherlock Holmes Pub

117

(among my other vices, I was a Holmesian), did the tourist things, and made arrangements to take the train up to Cambridge for my talk. This trip was uneventful, except for the unpleasant incident at High Table referred to at the beginning of the chapter. However, on the way back, I was waiting on the platform for my train back to London, when I heard a distant "chuff-chuff." With no announcement or fuss, out of the fog came a perfectly preserved British "Castle" class steam locomotive and maybe eight equally well preserved passenger cars. The train stopped, the engine crew got out and did a little oiling, reboarded, and the train sailed off into the fog. The curious thing was that nobody on the platform paid the slightest attention to this extraordinary sight. Maybe it really was a ghost train.

Castle class lokey out for a run.

Chapter 9
The First of the Great Adventures

After my round-the-world trip in 1979, rail travel settled into a routine of "commuting" several times a year to California and Detroit. I did make one vacation trip about this time to Pennsylvania to photograph the fabled Horseshoe Curve along the old Pennsylvania Railroad line through the Allegheny Mountains. This stretch of railroad, from Altoona to Johnstown is still one of the busiest in the United States, and well worth a visit by the even mildly serious railfan.

At the time of my visit, the actual railroad operating trains along the line was Conrail, although much of the equipment was still painted in the livery

Penn Central heavy freight at Horseshoe Curve, Pennsylvania.

of its predecessor, the Penn Central Although my primary purpose was railfanning, I was also trying out a new camera, one familiar to old-timey pro photographers but not many others. It was a Rolleiflex SL-66, and it took negatives that were 10 times bigger than 35mm. The resultant pictures could easily be blown up to mural size, with no loss of detail. It has only been within the last year or so that digital cameras have come close to equaling them .

GP-38, taken with Rollei SL-66.

In 1981 I was eligible for sabbatical leave. This often misunderstood part of university life is an absolute necessity for somebody who has to come up with new ideas as a way of making a living. Every once in a while you have to get away from the routine, see different ways of approaching something. Some folks like to go bury themselves in a research lab other than their own and take advantage of the time to concentrate on research they wouldn't have time to do back home. I took the opposite view. I wanted to do something completely different in as foreign an environment as I could find.

In shopping around for possibilities I stumbled on the Fulbright Exchange Program's listing of foreign faculty fellowships. One immediately jumped out. Xavier University, the little Jesuit school in the Philippines I had visited a year before, wanted somebody to teach college teachers how to teach; not just at Xavier, but as a "road show" that would travel all over the country. Had my name written all over it.

Fulbright faculty exchanges are one of the best (and cheapest) good will programs the State Department sponsors. I quickly found out that what you are *really* expected to do as a Fulbright Faculty Scholar is not the technical thing you are sent over for, but to be a counter to the negative impression about America and Americans that seems to have become the norm all over the world since the '60s. This meant that you were expected to get out and about, press the flesh, do favors, and in general be a good representative. Some Fulbright fellowships will take you to the Sorbonne or Oxford. Those are fiercely competitive. Those to, say, Botswana or Azerbaijan draw fewer applicants. As Mindanao island where Xavier University was located was an active combat area between the Philippine government and a long list of dissident rebels, including Muslim ones, I figured there wouldn't be too many fellowship candidates. I don't know if that was right, but I duly received an award.

The transpacific flight is long and tiring, no matter in what class you travel. The Philippines had the largest Fulbright program in Asia and was organized to greet new Fulbrighter's as we were known. I was told that I would be staying at the Las Palmas Hotel in the Malate/Ermita district of Manila until I could check in with the American Embassy, and that the hotel would send somebody to pick me up at the airport. The hotel was a hangout for Peace Corps volunteers, and was located in an "entertainment district" only a few blocks from the infamous Hobbit House bar which since 1973 has been staffed by what are today known as Little People.

121

Narcing.

When the plane came to a halt and everybody got off the chaos began, and lasted for the entire year. At first it was almost overwhelming. I didn't know where I was, or where to go. I eventually just flowed with the crowd to the arrivals area, and there I saw a guy holding a "Las Palmas Hotel" sign. He kind of looked like an Asian Al Capone. Elvis hairdo. Cigarette hanging out of the corner of his mouth.

"You are Dr. Heppner?" he asked. "Yes," I replied. "Come with me," he said. He picked up my bag, and we went out to the street. I got in the back seat of his ratty car, and he started navigating his way out of the terminal area. When we got out onto something looking like a normal street, he turned around and asked me,

"What kind of girl would you like for tonight?"

"What?"

"What kind of girl would you like tonight? Fat? Skinny? Maybe a dwarf?"

"Unh, no thanks, it was a really long flight and—.

"Ah, I know what you mean. Maybe you need a change of pace. How about a boy?'

"Thanks again, but–."

"Hash from the Mountain Province? Not like the shit you have in America."

"Yeah, sounds great, but I'm actually allergic to all that stuff."

He turned around again, and his eyes widened. "You are my first American guest who hasn't wanted at least *one* of my services. In that case, would you like to come to my house tonight for dinner and meet my family?"

That began a year of taking wild chances and not having any of them backfire. Well, *most* of them didn't backfire. I *did* go home with him and it was an absolutely charming experience. Turned out his name was Narciso (Narcing) Ayala, and I started a friendship with him that lasted many years beyond my stay. Narcing had an ulterior motive for his invitation, one that I would see a number of times during my visit. He had three children,

123

including a 19 year old daughter who attended the University of the Philippines. The PI (as it is often known there) is a very poor country, and snagging an American husband was like winning the lottery jackpot for a Filipino family. The daughter was lovely and gracious, but that wasn't in the cards for me, and Narcing was phlegmatic about it. I found out that he basically was a hustler, providing a decent living for his family by operating a number of slightly illicit businesses. One of his favorites was running organized sex tours for planeloads of Japanese businessmen. Cheating them blind was his way of taking a bit of revenge for the atrocities Japan committed against the Philippines during WWII. He and the girls liked them because they were organized and polite, quick, and tipped well. He also ran similar tours for Saudi rich guys, but he and the ladies didn't like them. Rich as they were, they never tipped. I later tried to compensate him for not marrying his daughter by hiring him for ridiculously high (by Philippine standards) prices to be my driver on my frequent trips to Manila.

I eventually found my way down to Cagayan de Oro City and Xavier University, a Jesuit college. They provided me with living quarters in the priests' residence. This would be my domicile for the next year and it was about as big as my freshman dorm room. I had my own toilet, but had to use a community shower with no hot water, but it didn't really matter because the daytime temperature averaged 95°, and the nighttime temperature was about 91°. There was no air conditioning. There was a leak in the sewer line, and earthworms would sometimes crawl out of the shower drain, but they didn't bite so I ignored them. My room was on the third floor, and I had a tiny balcony, on which every once in a while I'd find a Philippine cobra, which had climbed an overhanging tree, and dropped by for a howdy.

They also provided me with an administrative assistant, one of the single most competent people I ever met. Her name was Aurora (Ric-Ric) Gapuz, and she eventually became the university registrar. She arranged all my trips, made sure I didn't get myself killed doing something stupid out of ignorance, and helped me find trains.

I waited a discreet amount of time before telling her about my fetish for railroads. In general, Filipinos thought Americans were crazy in all aspects of life except making money, and I didn't want to reinforce the stereotype.

The Philippines were not a particularly fertile ground for railroading. There were over 7,000 separate islands, and 80 different language groups. Although the Philippines had been a Spanish colony for over 400 years, the Spanish rulers figured that if there were a common language, it would be easier for the people to revolt, so the priests and civil authorities all learned the local languages and the common folk were not permitted to learn Spanish. In the modern Philippines, the only places where Spanish was heard was in the high courts and in the homes of the rich descendants of the Spaniards. The same factors that prevented revolt also inhibited the construction of major, inter-island enterprises like railroads. However, when America took over as the Philippines' colonizer in 1898, one of our first steps was the establishment of universal English classes.

There had been plenty of very short mining, industrial, and agricultural railroads, most less than 10 miles long, but most of these had vanished before I arrived. By diligent search, Ric-Ric my assistant found a couple of choice survivors, and I am embarrassed to admit that a major factor in choosing which colleges I would visit was their proximity to a railroad.

Railroads were of little importance in general transportation in the PI. Far more significant were the ubiquitous "15 passenger Jeepneys." The Jeepneys were born after World War II, when as a reward to the Philippines for being one of our staunchest allies, we left all our vehicles behind instead of bringing them back home (I will not point out that in post-war assistance to our European allies, in contrast, we spent billions of dollars). We also "granted" the Philippines their independence in 1946, essentially saying, "Thanks for the help. See ya around. Good luck."

Jeepney. Probably wouldn't meet NTSB safety standards.

However this gesture was not quite as insignificant as it sounds. There is a national personality characteristic that the Filipinos ascribe to themselves called *remedios*. *Remedios* is the ability to fix things, and the Filipinos believe it is better to repair than to replace with new. So when they had these thousands of Jeeps, and a tremendous need for inter-village transportation, the Filipinos took the Jeeps, made homebuilt extended bodies, and presto, the "15 passenger Jeepney." However, you hardly ever saw as few as 15 passengers. They were dual purpose vehicles, carrying both passengers and cargo.

As you moved into the interior, especially in the then-untouched old forest areas, transportation was whatever would carry you. On one trip to central Mindanao I made with an Xavier anthropologist, the only "public" transportation was huge Peterbilt logging trucks, which would soon be covered like an anthill with riders.

Transportation in the interior. Note the unobserved "No Riders" sign on the bumper. Note also the guy with the carbine, our "guide" as we moved deeper into rebel-held country.

The first visit I scheduled for the express purpose of riding trains was to Panay Island and the Panay Island Railway (PIR). The PIR was a 60 mile long 42" gauge railroad that had been built in 1905, and operated on-and-off til 1985. There was some mining along the way, which probably accounted for the building of the railroad in the first place. It ran between the cities of Iloilo and Roxas City.

When I visited, the railroad was on its last legs. It still operated freight service using some decrepit Japanese diesels, and had a couple of passenger trains a day. These were perhaps the most remarkable trains I've seen in many miles of travel.

They were essentially handmade by a man named Florencio Unson Jr. who took the bones of three abandoned International Harvester R185

Panay Island Railroad terminal at IloIlo City.

trucks, and reassembled the moving parts onto some old sugar cane flatcars, that had used railroad trucks left behind by the Japanese when they fled in 1945. The transmission from the IH trucks was preserved, thus this was the only train I am aware of with a gearshift lever. He then built the bodies of the cars out of wood and metal. The construction did not engender a good deal of confidence. You had to jump between the cars while the train was moving if you wanted to go from car to car, so most folks were content with their first seats. It proved too difficult to provide brakes in this cobbled up arrangement, so the train had none, and you had to jump on or off at intermediate stations because the train didn't stop–it coasted into the terminals. This was *remedios* at its finest.

My next train ride was on the Philippine National Railways in Luzon, the big island on which is the capital, Manila. At one time, the

Panay Island coupler.

Intermediate station boarding on the Panay Railway.
The first car is the "locomotive."

PNR operated almost 300 miles of track from the southeast at Legaspi City through Manila to San Fernando in the north, but due to earthquake, typhoon, flooding, volcano, mismanagement, and squatters settling on the track, much of the system has been cut back, although there is a thriving commuter system around Manila.

In 1982, the train still ran from Manila to the northernmost point on the line, San Fernando, which had been the end point of the Bataan Death March during WWII. Ric-Ric had scheduled me for a visit to University of the Northern Philippines in Vigan, whose President was, strangely enough, the sister of Philippine President Ferdinand Marcos. I'm sure the staff of UNP was scratching their collective heads at my choice of transportation, because there was perfectly good scheduled air service to Vigan, and they had to send a car and driver down to pick me up, a round trip of 150 miles. But, what can you do, Americans–.

Vigan was charming, one of the most perfectly preserved cities in the world still dominated by Spanish colonial architecture. Local transport was provided by horse-drawn cabs called *calesas*, which were not there for the tourists, but provided practical everyday transportation.

It was in Vigan that I had one of the landmark experiences of my Philippine year. One of the bonuses of my tour of duty was that when I visited a new provincial college, it was sort of a big deal for them to have a foreign visitor so there was almost always a banquet and a cultural show for the guest. In Vigan, at the banquet I was

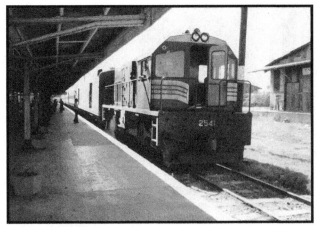

Philippine National Railways train at San Fernando.

seated between Madame President and the resident Archbishop. Toward the beginning of the meal, a waiter brought out a bowl of–how shall I say this?–stuff. His Grace turned to me and said, "Ah, this is a local delicacy called *papaitan*. It is like paté. Here, let me prepare it for you." He broke off a piece of bread, buttered it with the *papaitan*, and handed it to me. I thanked him and popped it in my mouth. I was struck dumb. No words can describe what it tasted like. My eyes widened, and it took me a few seconds to be able to speak. Finally, I said, "Your Grace, I don't believe I've ever tasted anything like this!" He smiled with delight, and said "I'm so glad you liked it! Here, have another." Remembering the Asian injunction against refusing gifts, I accepted it and somehow got it down without puking. Sometimes you have to make sacrifices for international friendship.

After I got back to Cagayan de Oro City, I asked Ric-Ric, whose family was from the province where Vigan is located, what *papaitan* was. Her eyes bugged out, and she said, "Oh, no! They should have known better than to serve you that. I will scold my cousin who arranged the trip."

"Ric, what is *papaitan*?"

"You do not want to know."

"I have to know. It's part of the experience."

"Oh, if you insist. When they slaughter the goat, they take the contents of the small intestine, squeeze them out, and then marinate them in bile from the gall bladder. It is very nutritious."

She was right; I shouldn't have asked.

After the *papaitan*, the train ride back to Manila was an anticlimax. The PNR train back to Manila was, ironically given the history of the Philippines, composed primarily of well-used, cast-off Japanese equipment. From Manila, it was the overnight boat back to Cagayan de Oro.

Sugar cane burning locomotive.

I've saved the best for last. Once it became known around Xavier that I was interested in trains, especially steam locomotives, stories came back to me that on the island of Negros (pronounced nay-gross), there still were operating steam engines working the sugar plantations. They were fueled by, of all things, sugar cane.

Negros was dominated by huge sugar cane plantations and a

correspondingly large number of sugar mills which refined sugar from the harvested cane. One of the largest was Victorias Central, on the northern side of the island, and as I discovered, it had a fleet of beautifully maintained and colorful two-foot gauge steam engines used to pull the cars full of sugar cane.. Most of them were German Henschel 0-8-0 tank engines, with auxiliary tenders to carry the huge loads of sugar cane fuel. There were also a couple of engines made by Baldwin, which had made similar engines for plantations around the world. Ric-Ric had arranged the trip for me, and she must have "known a guy" because I had the run of the place, and they ran all the engines that were under steam out of their shed for me to take pictures.

I was very sad to leave the Philippines when the year was up. Oddly, I found it more difficult to re-adjust to life back home than to adjust to life there, exotic as it was compared to my normal US existence. For example, in a poor country, you don't have the choices about almost anything that you do in the US. For instance, if you wanted a beer, you got San Miguel. If you wanted a soft drink, you got a Coke. In a restaurant, you got the chicken or the pork. Pretty soon that become normal. When I got back to the States, my first day in San Francisco, I went to a restaurant on Polk Street, and got into this surrealistic conversation.

"May I bring you something to drink?"
"Yes, thank you. A beer."
"What kind of beer?"
Confused. "What kind of beer?"
Annoyed. "Yes. Bottled? Draft?"
"I don't know. Bottled."
"What kind?"
"I don't know. Any kind."
"Sir, I can't bring you any kind. We have 25 different kinds. You'll have to tell me."

Freaking out. "Just bring me a &^%$^& beer!"

We got through that, but then I thought she was going to call the cops on me when she asked what I would like for lunch, and I said, "Meat."

I had a little 250cc Yamaha motorcycle in Cagayan de Oro (huge by Philippine standards). Once I hit San Francisco, I was in no hurry to get back to the east coast, so I somehow got the idea that it would be a bit of an adventure to buy a Harley in San Francisco (with 6 times the engine displacement) and drive across country. Just like "Easy Rider." So I went down to the local Harley dealer, Dudley Perkins, and explained to the salesman that I'd never driven anything bigger than a 250, but I'd like to buy something like a Harley Low Rider FX and drive it across the US. Fortunately for me, the salesman instantly figured out that this would be insanity, but instead of embarrassing me, suggested that he check one out. I could then tag along as a passenger to see what it would be like.

He grabbed one, I climbed on board, he instantly did as close as a Low Rider could do to a wheelie, and then practically with the speed of light, shot onto the Bayshore Freeway. I had never been so scared in my life. After about 15 minutes, he came back to Van Ness Avenue, and helped me off. This required some effort, because my legs were locked in place. I thanked him profusely, walked across the street, caught a Market Street streetcar, went down the Western Pacific Railroad office, bought a ticket on the next day's *California Zephyr,* and didn't get back on a motorcycle for another 10 years.

When I got back to the University of Rhode Island I quickly realized what a difference an almost unlimited supply of very cheap labor means. As a visiting faculty member at Xavier, I had an administrative assistant. The administrative assistant had two secretaries. Each of the secretaries had a "go-fer" to run errands. All at my beck and call. They would run personal errands for me, like buying shirts in town–basically anything that would

133

allow me to spend 100% of my time on the thing I was supposed to do when I was over there. Great system. But within hours of my starting back to work in Rhode Island, I had more or less settled into my office, but then had some paperwork that had to go over to a Dean's office. I took it to our department secretary and said, "Sandy, could you run this over to the Dean's office for me?" She looked at me as if I had grown an additional head, handed it back to me, and said, "Welcome home." Sandy had had experience with returning sabbatical profs.

I soon got back into the routine of classes, administrative squabbles, late nights at the lab, and squadrons of grad students. It didn't take me long, though, to start thinking about the next train trip.

Chapter 10

A Wee Bit 'O This, And a Wee Bit 'O That

The '80s were a kind of miscellaneous decade, trainwise, for me. I did a lot of traveling, but much of it was routine, on routes I had ridden many times before. I was also doing a lot more air travel as rail destinations in the U.S. went into the history books, or became impractical for train travel. For example, lovely as it is, Fargo, North Dakota is served by two trains a day, which now have arrival and departure times between midnight and three AM; whereas, when I went there for bird meetings in the early '70s, the times were much more convenient. There were other trips which were enormously interesting or exciting, like Israel in 1986 just after the Berlin discothèque bombing which killed two American GI's, but they didn't involve any rail travel.

The decade was not entirely barren, however. I had a wonderful undergraduate student who worked in my laboratory, and after his graduation, we became friends. His name was Tom Chrostek, and he was a farm boy (yes, such things exist in Rhode Island) from the northwestern part of the state. We shared interests in agriculture and military history, an odd combination, I'll admit. He was strong as an ox, and in return for my letting him keep his horses on my land, he cleared about 2 acres of bull briars with a machete (for those of you unfamiliar with bull briar, it is like green barbed wire).

Tom's grandmother had given him a generous graduation present, and I had a bunch of frequent flier miles, so we decided to take a trip to a place that has a fascinating and concentrated military history; Scotland. By strange happenstance, it also is LOADED with early railroad history.

The trip took several months in the planning, because we had to do a tremendous amount of reading to narrow down where we'd go. I had one of my regular trips to San Francisco scheduled during this period, and I decided to look up an old high school friend, Diana, whose stepfather was an old Scot. I figured I'd ask him for suggestions.

Diana's family lived in a stunning home near Golden Gate Park. Her stepfather was Sir John B. deC. M. Saunders, M.D. FRCS, retired Dean of the Medical School of the University of California, San Francisco. He was in his early 80's at the time. Diana invited me to dinner and after the meal was over, with a certain amount of trepidation (because he was a VERY intimidating man), I told Dr. Saunders I was planning a military history of Scotland trip and did he have any suggestions?

At this, his eyes lit up, he excused himself from table, said, "I'll be back," and went upstairs. After about 10 minutes, he came back down clad in full Highlands regalia; kilt, doublet, sporran (belt pouch), dirk (ceremonial dagger), and sgian dubh (sock knife).

I would like to think my jaw didn't drop at this apparition, as it would have been impolite, but I was quite speechless. Dr. Saunders sat down, faced me, and said in a very heavy Scots' brogue (acquired during his education at Edinburgh; he had been born in South Africa), "Young man, the farst thing ye must know, is that every Scot is barn wi' a taste for cold steel," and slammed his dirk on the table. He was right; check out Mel Gibson's "Braveheart." He then proceeded to give a one-hour dissertation on Scottish battle history, with visitation suggestions (which Tom and I followed pretty closely).

The basic plan was to travel up to the National Railway Museum in York in the Midlands, and detour to the west to ride the lovely little Welch narrow gauge mountain railroads, of which the most famous was the Ffestiniog. Then back to the mainline, and up to Edinburgh. From Edinburgh, it was northward to Inverness which was the base for our battlefield explorations, reaching it by traveling across the fabled Firth of Forth bridge. In Inverness, we could do a spot of Loch Ness Monster investigation. Out of Inverness, it was the stunning Kyle of Lochalsh line to the namesake town, from which one could take a short ferry ride to the Isle of Skye, which is possibly the most romantic place name in the world (other than Casablanca, of course).

There are some wonderful railroad museums around the globe, and fortunately, we have some in the United States that are international class. The California Railroad Museum in Sacramento comes to mind, as does the Baltimore and Ohio in (where else) Baltimore. However, for sheer jaw-droppingness, it would be hard to beat the British National Railway Museum in York. Britain has a number of outstanding smaller rail museums, particularly the one in Crewe, but York is the stellar attraction. Although they've had to cut back in recent years, the outstanding feature of York was the fact that so much of their equipment was in operating condition, and in fact, was regularly run on the main lines.

From York, we detoured west on British Rail to the Welch town of

Merddin Emrys; adorable locomotive.

Porthmadog, about 20 miles from the top of Snowdon, Wales' highest mountain peak. Porthmadog lies in juxtaposition to "Snowdonia," the heart of Wales' slate mining area. Slate has been both quarried and mined here since the 1200's. Porthmadog is only about 50 miles from Pen-y-Darren, where the world's first steam railway locomotive was built by Richard Trevithick, and used to haul iron over a 10 mile tramway.

Today, Snowdonia is the locale of ten narrow gauge steam tourist railways, mostly former mining or quarry lines. Our destination was the Ffestiniog Railway, now the Ffestiniog and West Highlands Railway. The sterling feature of the Ffestiniog was its locomotives. The locomotive pulling our train was the *Merddin Emrys* built in 1879, and one of the more unusual types of locomotives, a "double Fairlie." This design was the ancestor of the modern diesel locomotive, where power was delivered to the rails not by large, centralized driving wheels like a conventional steam engine, but by two small engines powering wheels at the ends of the locomotive. The Welch narrow gauge lines are about two feet between rails, and the locomotives look like they should have "Thomas" painted on them. Such cuteness would normally inspire a gag reflex in a railfan, but these little guys are *legitimately* adorable, and you just wanted to hug them.

After Wales, it was back to the Midlands mainline to continue the journey to Edinburgh. It was drizzly and chill when we got there (surprise!), and we arrived at dinnertime, so naturally we had to find someplace that would serve us a *haggis,* even though it was not the week of January 25, when this traditional dish is served at dinners commemorating the great Scottish poet, Robert Burns.

Dear Reader, you have already been introduced to *papaitan*, the revolting traditional dish of the Philippines. Haggis is its Celtic cousin. A proper haggis is made of the minced "pluck" from a sheep carcass (heart, liver, lungs) mixed with oatmeal, suet and spices, then stuffed in a sheep's stomach and simmered for several hours. As served, it looks something like a small, greasy, greyish-brown football with pipes sticking out of either end. Fortunately, the traditional drink accompanying haggis is Scotch whiskey. Neither Tom nor I were particularly big distilled spirits drinkers, but we found a couple of shots extremely helpful before making that first slice.

Sláinte!

Next day, we toured a distillery in the morning (not a terrific idea) and spent several days doing tourist things around Edinburgh, which is a lovely, grey city. It was while wandering about that I made an observation whose sequellae have plagued me ever since. I love to travel. I love to try to take good pictures. But if you're traveling and concentrating on the good shots, you tend not to be aware of much outside your viewfinder. Conversely, if you are chatting up the locals, and trying to concentrate on the very informative tour guide; you miss your best shots. So it really is often an either/or. Do you maximize the travel experience, or concentrate on the camera? That, I believe, now explains why I have so few pictures of this trip. I was having too much fun with the traveling.

After several days, it was time for the train to Inverness, which was the northernmost point of the trip. Although the route is pleasant enough, passing mostly through agricultural and foothill country, there is one feature that should put this route on every railfan's bucket list. That is the crossing of the Forth Railroad Bridge, across the estuary (or "firth") of the Forth River, a few miles outside the city of Edinburgh.

The Forth Railroad Bridge was completed in 1890, and was the first major structure in Great Britain to be built primarily of steel. It is a three-span cantilever bridge. One's first impression upon seeing it is one of engineering overkill. It is *massive*. Trains that cross it are dwarfed. This is not an accident. Another major Scottish railway bridge crossing the Firth of Tay had collapsed in a windstorm in 1879, just as a train passed over, sending the train and its 75 passengers into watery graves. The Tay bridge was built on the cheap, and was rather delicate looking. When the Forth Railroad Bridge was commissioned, mindful of public opinion, its engineers, Sir Benjamin Baker and Sir John Fowler, took the opposite tack, and followed the Harley-Davidson motto, "You can't go wrong, if it's big and strong." Unfortunately, the approaches to the bridge follow a straight line to the structure, so as a passenger, you can't get the full effect, but as you cross, you can see that the girders that it is composed of are huge.

Inverness was the jumping off point for the rest of our side trips. Although it had nothing to do with trains, Loch Ness was only a short bus ride from the city, and then you could take a little tour boat down the lake.

I have to admit–although I'm a scientist and a skeptic-Loch Ness was *spooky*. Or maybe *creepy*. It is 26 miles long, a mile wide, about 700 feet deep and full of underwater caves. Lots of stuff could hide there–assuming that there was something there that needed hiding. The water is loaded with peat, so that it appears almost black. Your hand disappears if you stick it in the water. Not helping is that the shoreline is dotted with old ruined castles that look like they came from "Lord of the Rings." I half expected Smaug to pop up and roast the boat.

Urquhart Castle on Loch Ness.

Then it was time to do what had been the original major purpose of the trip, but had somehow been sidetracked, as it were-- visiting notable locations of Scottish military history. By now, we had little time left, and selected a famous battleground named Culloden near Inverness that marked the end of the Jacobite rebellion that attempted to restore Roman Catholic rulers to the throne of the United Kingdom.

The battle of Culloden took place in 1746 between Scottish highland clansmen and their allies, the English Stuarts led by "Bonnie Prince Charlie," (Charles Edward Stuart), and English Hanoverian Protestants led by the Duke of Cumberland. As battlefields go, it is not particularly large, but like other noted fields of combat I've visited, like Antietam and Gettysburg, it has a somber and dismal atmosphere, a stillness that reflects the dreadful things that happened there.

It was an appropriately bleak and drizzly day. Tom and I had both read John Prebble's excellent book on Culloden, and were able to self-guide. We were both struck here and at other Scottish locations with how harsh and unforgiving the landscape was. You would have to be very tough to survive here in a pre-machine age. Perhaps that's why the Scots excelled at civil and mechanical engineering for so many years. Without machinery, you would have to lead a barely survivable lifestyle.

Appropriately sobered, we returned to Inverness for the last leg of the trip, on the former Inverness and Ross-shire, and the Dingwall and Skye Railway to the Kyle of Lochalsh in the west of Scotland. While in the train station in Inverness, we spotted Scotland's version of the *Orient Express*, the *Royal Scotsman* waiting for passengers. Tom and I were reasonably well dressed, and were able to wander over to the train like we belonged there. It featured beautifully restored '20s cars, and was sometimes pulled by a steam engine. The stellar attraction of the train was an enclosed observation/parlor car at the end of the train, in which you could slowly sip a wee dram of Glenfarclas 1955 as you watched the country roll by in an increasingly dense fog.

Royal Scot cars.

Kyle of Lochalsch observation car.

That luxury, however, was not for us. We took the regular Kyle of Lochalsch train, but did spring a bit extra for the observation car. *Our* observation car looked like it had been converted from an old Red Line subway car from Boston, but the view out the back window was just as nice as the one the swells on the *Royal Scotsman* enjoyed. The train slowly wound through a river valley, then slithered along the edge of a spectacular estuary, finally ending on a dock at the edge of the village, from which you could see the Isle of Skye about a mile away. Now there is a bridge that connects Skye with the mainland, but on our trip there was a ferry between the two sides of the channel. There was plenty of time before the train returned to Inverness, so we hopped over to Skye for lunch and a sampling of Skye's most noted whisky, Talisker. That marked the end of the trip, and we retraced our steps back to London as directly as possible.

The Kyle of Lochalsch. Skye in the distance.

Alas, there is a sad ending to this story. I kept in touch with Tom after the trip. He returned to his home town in the northwest of Rhode Island and resumed his farm career, but he also picked up a teaching certificate, and became a high school history teacher. He married one of my former teaching assistants, and had two strapping boys. He became very active in community affairs. Although he was enormously strong, he had always had intermittent and rather odd health problems. He was ultimately diagnosed with leukemia, and after a long struggle, it got the best of him in his 40th year. Almost a thousand people visited during calling hours, and his friends, many of whom were master craftsmen, built his coffin out of local pine. It was strong, straight, and true. Just like the man. I miss him.

In 1988, I found myself back in Japan, this time as a tourist. The destination to the south was Kyoto, a can't miss for anyone interested in Japanese art and culture, and Sapporo, on the island of Hokkaido to the north, where I had friends. This destination also provided an excuse for riding through the newly-opened Seikan railway tunnel connecting the islands of Honshu and Hokkaido under the Tsugaro Strait. This tunnel was at the time the longest and deepest undersea tunnel in the world.

The entry point for most visitors to Japan from the west is Tokyo. The city is almost overwhelming for new visitors not on some sort of escorted party. It's as if all of Manhattan was like Times Square. I had a couple of days before heading south, so one of the first stops was the Transportation Museum in Chiyoda Prefecture. I did eventually try the subway system, but the basic way western visitors get around is to tell the desk clerk in the hotel where you want to go, he or she scribbles something on a piece of paper, you go out front, hail a cab, and give the cabbie the piece of paper. Most cabbies who call at hotels know how to get to the usual tourist sites, but the Transportation Museum was not one of them, so there was much head scratching, conversations with pedestrians, and finger pointing.

Eventually I arrived (providentially, the hotel had given me ANOTHER piece of paper for a taxi with instructions back to the start. If I had lost that, I'd probably still be in Japan). The first impression while walking toward the building was startling. The structure itself was totally unremarkable, and looked like a medium sized office building. However, at one end, they had sawed off the front 15 feet or so of a Hikari bullet train and an old steam engine, and backed them up to the wall, so it looked like the engines were bursting out of the building. Your first thought was, "My God! There's been a terrible accident here!" You took a second look, ha, ha, joke's on me. It was a good, not a great museum, mostly because it was crammed into a relatively small building in the middle of the city. It has subsequently moved to larger quarters.

After a day or so, I felt confident enough to wander around the neighborhood, and it didn't take long to realize that I was in a totally different culture. This manifested itself in a number of ways, particularly in a distinctive form of English called, usually with some degree of affection, Japlish, or Engrish. It is a combination of mistranslation, odd syntax, creative spelling, and just plain, "What the–????" Even multinational companies, which ought to have native English speakers at their beck and call, sometimes lapse. Coke's big slogan at the time was, "I

And it feels so *good!*

feel Coke!" *Feel* Coke? One of the most popular soft drinks was and is Pokari "Sweat," a sports drink.

It seems like half of Tokyo lies underground, and every once in a while, as you're passing through the maze of corridors and subterranean malls, you pass something that looks very much like a blast door in a missile launch facility. Perhaps something to do with earthquakes or maybe long memories from 1945.

Hikari getting ready to boogie.

The Hikari train for Kyoto leaves from Tokyo Station, which handles about 3,000 trains a day (compared to about 1,200 trains a day in Penn Station). Eventually, I found my way to the platform, and again noted the car numbers and lines painted such that boarding passengers would be lined up exactly where their car door would be when the train stopped. The ride on the Hikari train was as expected; very smooth, and frankly, somewhat boring.

After three or four days in Kyoto, a great experience, it was time to return to Tokyo and change stations for the train to Sapporo.

Getting to Sapporo by train was a reasonably complex operation. Although there is now an east coast Shinkansen line in the north of Honshu, it operates on standard gauge tracks, whereas the through trains from Toyko to Sapporo through the Seikan tunnel operate on Japanese narrow gauge. This northern Shinkansen line also operates what are, with little argument, the ugliest high speed trains in the world. One looks like Daffy Duck from the front, and the other appears to have Elephant Man warty syndrome. However, when I took my trip the preferred way to travel was on the older line so you didn't have to change trains.

In 1988 Japan still operated a fairly extensive network of first class, all sleeping car overnight trains called "blue trains," for their color. In concept, these were more like the old *Twentieth Century Limited, or Super Chief*, than the *Orient Express*. Their clientele was primarily business travelers. To mark the the opening of the Seikan Tunnel, they started a new blue train called the *Hokutosei*, or "Big Dipper." The Japanese seem to like to name things after constellations, for no apparent reason. "Subaru" means "The Pleiades." Following Gresham's Law, which says the bad drives out the good, the blue trains have not fared well with the advent of cheap air fares, regardless of how uncomfortable the flying experience is. Even the crash of Japan Airlines flight 123 in 1985, which killed 520 people after a horrific 32 minute terror ride did not dissuade the bargain hunters, and now there are only a few blue trains left and those that do survive are more luxury than business trains.

But that was all ahead. The *Hokutosei* was a beautiful modern train, not ostentatious, but efficient and everything in good taste. The dining car served French or Japanese food, your choice. After dinner, the dining car converted itself into a Pub Car, and conviviality reigned until closing.

The highlight of this trip was the passage through the Seikan tunnel, which is 33 miles long, 15 of which are under the ocean. At its deepest, it is 790 feet below sea level, which is about the collapse depth of a WWII German submarine. There are two underwater "stations" which have platforms and vertical shafts for emergency exits. When the *Hokutosei* was

148

new, it would stop at one of the stations, even though it was the middle of the night, so passengers could get off and try not to think about the fact that the wall of the tunnel was under 220 pounds per square inch of water pressure. Naturally, I had to get off and experience this. Although you couldn't *feel* the pressure, in the sense of having your ears hurt, you were *aware* of the fact that a pinhole sized hole in the wall of the tunnel would produce a stream of water that could effortlessly saw you in half. Not pleasant. The floor of Tsugaru Strait is littered with the bones of Japanese ships sunk by the U.S. Navy in the last days of World War II. I wondered if any of them lay across the route of the tunnel. More ghosts.

Sapporo was a charming small city ("small" in Japan is a population of about two million), the site of the 1972 Winter Olympics, and there were structural reminders of the glory days of those Olympics everywhere. Sapporo has a modest claim to culinary fame. Miso ramen, the impoverished student's salvation until Mom's next check comes through was developed here. Its *real* claim to fame is the inimitable Sapporo Beer.

After a couple of delightful days hosted by friends, it was back to Tokyo for the long flight home. International flying was still pretty nice then, even in coach. The only downside was that smoking was still permitted on airplanes, although I don't know–I think I might now trade sitting next to a guy sucking on a Camel in exchange for four extra inches of leg room.

Chapter 11

The Main Line Gets Rebuilt

The year 1990 brought changes that were to have a dramatic effect on my rail travels. Early in the year, I gave a paper that brought me a certain amount of notoriety in scientific circles, markedly increasing the number of my speaking invitations which, of course, required more train travel. Then in midyear I abandoned the bachelor lifestyle I had gotten used to and which served me well for many years. Needless to say this was a big step, and not just *anyone* would be comfortable with the kind of adventuring I was accustomed to, and was unwilling to leave entirely.

I got lucky. When she was in her 20's, Marjorie had bicycled all the way across the United States, and early in her career as a forensic psychologist, she had gotten used to dealing with a fortunately rare class of upright citizen, your basic serial killer, cannibal, etc. So I figured a couple of complexities on train trips, should they happen, wouldn't faze her (I'll not mention very much more about her professional life here. In her current position, a discreet and low profile is required).

Then there was the matter of a proposal. Both of us loved corny old romantic movies, and the critical scene in *An Affair to Remember* where Cary Grant was going to propose to Deborah Kerr on the top of the Empire State Building seemed like the perfect one to emulate. So I booked lunch at the original *Four Seasons* restaurant in Manhattan and we took what had been the old New Haven *Colonial* from Rhode Island to New York.

It was an unusually hot day and I had the ring in my pocket. We walked the couple of blocks from Penn Station over to the Empire State, found the entrance to the observation deck, and– what the HELL?!? It was closed for repairs. Not a great beginning to a romantic proposal. Fortunately, she didn't know at this point it was going to BE a proposal. I hadn't told her

The beginning of the adventure.

what was on the agenda for the day, so she was only mildly disappointed; she thought it was just going to be a vacation day in the city. We caught a cab up to the *Four Seasons* and the Pool Room, had a typical magnificent lunch, and then when the waiter brought out the dessert, I went down on my knee in front of all the nabobs and movers and shakers, and made my pitch. Unlike some of the OTHER doofuses who propose in public places, and have the stunningly embarrassing experience of Charlene saying, "Oh Phil, that's such a wonderful thought, but–," I had the advantage of having ALREADY assured myself of a "yes," in a less elegant way back in Rhode Island.

Once it was official we had to decide on a honeymoon trip. Naturally there had to be Paris, but beyond that, how about the train? How about the adventure? Even though it wasn't really an "adventure," I wanted her to see Switzerland and the Alps, and that might be the place to start. I was still working with a travel agent, and she discovered something for us. There was a relatively new European luxury train called the *al Andalus Express* that was modeled after the resuscitated *Orient Express*. It made a week-long loop trip through Spain that cost about as much as the state of North Dakota would if it were on the open market. However, once in a while, it made an overnight trip from Malaga to Seville, and you could book it for a single day's trip. That was only about the price of Fargo.

But then, what do you do in Seville, after you've gotten a haircut? Hmmm. Seville is only about 100 miles from Gibralter and across the Strait of Gibralter is Tangier in Morocco. I'd never been to Africa, and Fes,

Morocco was the site of the world's oldest continuously operating educational institution, the University of al-Karaouine. A perfect place to visit for a college professor. So we decided to fly to Geneva, and then take the train to Africa.

The trip did not start well. We had booked business class on SwissAir, but they had seriously overbooked, and contrary to the usual situation, we were downclassed to coach, where we were sandwiched between a pair of moms with infants with very healthy lungs. As I look back on it, we had little to squawk about. The plane was a DC-10 and the seats were in a 2-4-2 configuration rather than the 3-4-3, and sometimes even 3-5-3 configuration sometimes found in widebodies today. I'm not sure how much legroom there was, but it was a LOT more than at present (unless my legs have somehow gotten longer as I've aged), and there was actually decent food rather than the hardtack, gruel, and fatbelly that is the norm now on international flights. The other thing that eased our pain is that after we arrived, they refunded our entire fare, not just the difference between coach

TGV's.

and business.

Geneva was lovely as always, but alas, the weather was crappy, and although we went to Zermatt, Marjorie didn't get to see the Matterhorn. We puttered around Geneva for a couple of days, then it was a TGV (*tres grande vitesse*) train to Paris, overnight sleeper train to Madrid, then regular Spanish train to Malaga, where we arrived at 6:35 PM. (In case you're wondering how I remembered the time; Marjorie saved the tickets).

Eighteen cars worth of decadence on the *al-Andalus*.

The *al-Andalus Express* was in the station when we arrived, and it was stunning. Eighteen cars long, all in rich dark red and cream with gilt accents. The cars were from the '20s and '30s, and had been mechanically brought up to contemporary standards. They were completely air conditioned, and could easily handle a hundred miles an hour, although that wasn't the idea.

It wasn't until we boarded at 8:00 PM that we discovered that there were only 8 passengers on board, but a full crew. Normally, this was a

The Countess awaits her Lafite '61.
We wish.

maintenance move, but the company had just decided that a few passengers, even at a steep discount, was better than no passengers and our travel agent had somehow heard about it.

We settled into our marquetry-decorated compartment, when the *chef de train* dropped by and asked if the *chef de cuisine* might speak to us. Of course, he could. Chef explained that there was no menu, but if he might make a few suggestions, and they met with our approval, he would have time to shop for fresh ingredients at a nearby market before we left at 10:00 PM, and dinner would be shortly after that. *Si*, that would be satisfactory.

Dinner was at 10:00 PM, just after departure. The service was impeccable. It should have been; there were only four other diners. After dinner, we still had a bit of energy, so a touch of dancing was in order. We strolled down to the Discotheque-Piano Bar car *Giralda*, where there was a jazz trio. We danced enough to work up a sweat, so our next stop was the Shower Car, where there was a little sign that read, "In the waiting area as you enter the shower car, you will see a meter indicating both the water temperature and which shower units are free."

Next day, still somewhat in a state of stupor, we got off in Seville. We stayed overnight, and set out the following morning in a local train to Algeciras, the last Spanish stop before Gibralter. The train was nothing special but before long, we encountered the most unexpected part of the whole trip.

Although Algeciras is almost due south of Seville, the train instead headed southeast through rolling farmland until it came to a rail junction town named Bobadilla. The line then branched off to the southwest, running through increasingly steep foothills, and eventually into a river canyon. I later discovered that the river was the Rio Guadiaro, and it ran through the Spanish Sierra Nevada mountains in Andalucia.

Before long, I realized that this was one of the great unsung rail river runs of the world, and I'd never heard of it. Even today, it is little known apart from British rail buffs (The line was built by the British in 1890 to provide access for the Gibralter garrison and their families to summer hotels with a more hospitable climate than Gibralter's summer sauna. Much like the Darjeeling line in India). It had a lot of the feeling of the Denver and Rio Grande run through the Colorado River canyons; steep cliffs on one side of the tracks, 1,000 foot vertical drops off the other.

al-Andalus cabin.

The train arrived in early afternoon in Algeciras. Our Gibralter ferry was not scheduled to leave for several hours, and as it was a Sunday, everything was closed. Everything. I took every possible picture around the station,

155

and after having exhausted that source of amusement, the only thing left was a hardcover copy of a biography of the Polaroid film inventor, Edward Land, I had providentially brought with me. It didn't take long to finish and as there was nothing else to do, I re-read it. Land was a remarkable man, but I don't care if I ever hear about him again.

Not southern Rhode Island.

Finally, it was time to leave and catch the ferry to Tangier. As soon as we got aboard, we had a "not in Kansas anymore," experience. Although most passengers were wearing western clothing, there was a scattering of *djellabas, kaftans,* and *fezes* on some of the passengers. After an uneventful crossing, the landing at the port of Tangier was the barely controlled chaos that was normal in the non-Western world. As we debarked, I kept an eye on Marjorie to see how she was handling the confusion. Was this trip going to turn out to be a Really Bad Idea? Naaah, rolled off her like water off the proverbial duck's back. I guess working with guys who could have been the prototype for Hannibal Lecter was good preparation for the hubble-bubble of Tangier.

A guy from the hotel met us after we cleared customs, and we avoided much of the port arrival confusion. The hotel was your basic Arabian Nights tourist fantasy, but it was lovely, comfortable, and just what we needed after getting-on, getting-off, getting-on trains for the previous several days.

The following day we took a taxi down to the Tangier *ville* station. French and Arabic were the two languages of commerce, and Marjorie's memory of French proved invaluable. We found our train easily, and I had the first of a number of rail surprises on this run.

The train was made of older European-style compartment cars, with first and second class coaches. The track was standard gauge, and up front was a relatively modern EMD GL22C diesel locomotive, which is made in a variety of places around the world. I could see that there were overhead

Moroccan locomotive.

catenary lines; the route from Tangier to Fes was completely electrified. As we passed through engine and freight yards, I was somewhat astounded to see so many large heavy-duty electric and diesel freight locomotives. I later discovered that Morocco is the third largest producer of mineral phosphates (used for fertilizer or gunpowder) in the world and that accounted for the need for industrial-strength motive power.

The ride to Fes only took a couple of hours, and passed through a mostly agricultural landscape, dotted with flocks of sheep and their shepherds, and strings of scrawny pack mules. Looked positively biblical. Passing stations which had boards indicating the next train to Casablanca reminded us that we were not far from the scene of the first invasion of Patton's 3rd Army in the march toward the recapture of Europe by the Allies. Of course, it didn't hurt that one of the great romantic movies of all time was also named *Casablanca*, and that pretty soon, we too would "have Paris."

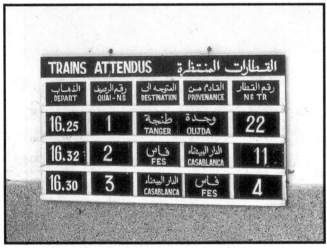

Moroccan train board.

Fes was way off the beaten path for American tourists and the majority of European tourists were French speakers. Not surprising, since Morocco had been a French colony. So the town was relatively "pure" and untouristy. In the Philippines I had lived in close proximity to a large Muslim population, and so was not unprepared for the local customs and courtesies. The ancient university I

View out the window on the way to Fes.

had come to see had taught not only secular subjects, but contained within its walls a *madrassa*, or religious school. There was thus some sensitivity about where non-Muslims could visit, so Marjorie and I engaged a guide to both show us the sights and keep us out of trouble, both of which he did admirably.

Before we started out on our visit to the *medina*, the ancient marketplace, I explained to the guide that we were experienced travelers, and knew that guides traditionally made part of their income by getting kickbacks from the shop owners they steered their guests to. However, we didn't have all that much time, and I told him I would pay him, in advance, what he would have made from the shopkeepers if he skipped that part of the process. He agreed enthusiastically.

He gave us a great tour but after several hours of walking around in the baking heat, we were tired, and asked Achmed to take us back to the hotel, because we were totally lost. Now, in these old markets you can't really tell whether you are indoors or in the street, because the streets are heavily covered with screens. So we kept going indoors-outdoors-indoors as Achmed took shortcuts. After what seemed like hours, we paused in what appeared to be an inside room covered by rugs. I immediately smelled a rat.

"Achmed!" I exclaimed. "I thought I said no stores."

"Ah, but Sir," he replied. "You said you wished to learn about the culture of Morocco, and you cannot separate the history of Morocco from the history of the rug. Mr. Mukherjee, the owner of the store, is an international expert on Moroccan rugs, and it will be his pleasure to instruct you. Please be seated. Mint tea?"

Mr. Mukherjee, an extremely well dressed Moroccan came out and introduced himself. Before he got too far, I explained to him that we had no interest in buying rugs, that I was but a schoolteacher (technically correct), we had spent our entire budget on the trip, and much as we thought his rugs were beautiful and we would treasure his teaching, we had no intention of buying (also technically correct, but we hadn't yet started on souvenirs).

He shrugged as if to say, "You insult me by suggesting that I might try to sell you a rug, when my mission is like yours, education." He then went on to give a brilliant discussion of the role of the rug in history and philosophy. Then Marjorie made a mistake.

I need to explain here that although many Americans *hate* bargaining, I *love* it. It is a contest of will and wit, and any deal that goes to conclusion is automatically a good deal for both parties.

The error Marjorie made was to admire a particularly fine small rug that was the subject of Mr. Mukherjee's current conversation. As soon as she said it, Mr. Mukherjee clapped his hands together, turned to me with a huge smile, and said, "Sir, we have a saying in Arabic that translates into English, 'Blessed by the Holy Prophet is he whose wife has good taste (I looked this up later-there actually is an Arabic proverb that is more-or-less like this).' Your wife has unerringly selected the most beautiful rug in our collection!"

Well, it *was* awfully nice, so I sent a tentative shot across his bow. "Not that I have the ability to buy something like that, but just so I can get some

160

idea of how such a thing would fit in a typical household budget, what would you ask for it?"

He smiled, knowing that the first guy to name a price loses, rubbed his hands together, and said, "Ah, Sir, it would be pointless to quote you a price because that rug has already been spoken for by the curator of the museum in Marakesh." Just then, a flunky came in and whispered something in his ear.

"What?" he exclaimed. "That ungrateful scoundrel! Sir, this is incredible. That was Marakesh. The Director has reneged on his promise to acquire the rug for the museum. So now I can sell it to you for only a thousand dollars, U.S."

"Ah, Mr. Mukherjee, you have been most kind to us, but as I explained I am a teacher on a teacher's modest salary. I could never pay for that rug, even though I am amazed at your low price. I would have thought it would be five thousand at least. But any sum I could name would be so low it would be an insult to you, and a violation of your hospitality."

"I am not easily insulted, Sir. What would you give me?"

"If I take a day off the end of our trip to save money, hmmm, yes, I could give you fifty dollars."

"Fifty dollars! That would not cover my overhead for half a day! How would I feed my six children if I accepted that offer?"

We dueled on like this for quite some time, Marjorie becoming more impatient by the minute. Finally, we came to terms at about $350. I shook hands with him, and gave him a credit card, which he examined carefully. As he was writing the transaction up, I asked, "Mr. Mukherjee, it has been a pleasure doing business with you, and now may I ask how many children you actually have?"

"Two," he replied. "And I do hope, Doctor, that your Rolex is a source of solace to you in your poverty."

After this, the train back to Tangier was a bit of an anticlimax. Once we

161

recrossed the Strait of Gibralter and reached Algeciras in Spain again, we went more-or-less directly back to Paris *via* Barcelona. We took an overnight regular Spanish train, and had a 2nd class "tourist" sleeping compartment. This was about as far from the *al-Andalus Express* as you could get. The 2nd class compartments had 6 bunk beds, stacked three high. The person on top was uncomfortably close to the ceiling. As the train pulled out of our station, Marjorie and I had the middle and top bunks, and our companions were a mother and two infant children. We were a bit anxious about this arrangement, having visions of screaming children all night, but the kids were great. Cute as bugs and terrific sleepers.

This train had a point of notable rail interest. The standard Spanish train track has a gauge that is about six inches wider than "standard" gauge used in France and most of the rest of Europe. In the old days, this meant a change of trains at the French/Spanish border, but then some clever inventor developed wheels that could slide along the axle. So at the border, there was a machine that the train passed over that unlocked the wheels on their axles, slid them in to the French gauge, and relocked them. This meant travelers could travel between the major cities of Spain and Paris without changing trains.

The trains had another feature that has been mentioned in previous chapters. The trains were made by the Talgo corporation, and had the double novelty of being articulated, and with a pendulum suspension. "Articulated" in railroad car parlance means that the train's cars share trucks, and are permanently coupled together. Their pendular suspension permitted a faster run around curves.

We finished the trip with three days in Paris. Ah, Paris. Lovely as it is, from a rail standpoint, other than the magnificent stations featured in Martin Scorcese's brilliant animated film, *Hugo,* there isn't much of interest except its unusual rubber-tired subway lines. This system is shared with only a few cities, like Montreal and Mexico City. The disadvantages; higher energy consumption, more repairs, and more air pollution, seem to outweigh the advantages of a somewhat quieter and smoother ride, and the ability to handle steeper grades.

We did our best to relive the best bits of movies like *American in Paris, Sabrina, Funny Face, Charade, and Gigi,* I'd like to think with some success. Finally, after 3 weeks of more or less continuous train travel, it was time to go home, and this time Swiss Air did right by us, and we arrived back in the 'States refreshed and ready for yet another round of train travel.

We'll always have Paris.

Chapter 12

Back at the Ranch Again

Sometimes, great ideas appear, but inexplicably, never really catch on and die unlamented and forgotten. Remember BetaMax, that was much better than VHS tape? Or HD DVD discs, that were better than Blu-Ray?

One of the institutions that is very important to universities, but poorly understood outside the ivied walls is the "sabbatical." The opportunity for creative people to have a change of scene every once in a while and get exposed to new ideas and people is an essential part of a research university. The catch is, it is costly. Universities typically pay half a faculty member's salary while they're away for a year, AND often have to hire an academic peon to teach the missing prof's classes whilst he or she is away. Excellent idea, but expensive.

But then in the mid-'80s, somebody came up with the idea of a "National Faculty Exchange." I say somebody, because the idea has essentially disappeared from the net; no real hits on Google. The idea was you publish a list of senior research faculty members from all over the country. Post their research area, the courses they teach, where they are in their careers, etc. Then people shop through the list, looking for somebody who lives in someplace else that pretty much does what they do. Then you *swap jobs* for a semester. Your home university continues to pay your salary, but has somebody else, in theory of equal quality, doing your job. No additional expense for the university.

Ideally, you'd swap other things as well. House. Car. Pets. The beauty is that the idea had all the benefits of a sabbatical, but none of the expense. Obviously too sensible to last.

In 1993, I was eligible for a sabbatical, but somebody gave me a copy of the National Faculty Exchange. I browsed through the "biology" entries, and one jumped out and grabbed me. A guy on the faculty in the Department of Zoology at New Mexico State University in Las Cruces named Walt Whitford. And he had a Rhode Island connection! He got his Ph.D. here in 1964. Maybe he'd like to come back to the old stomping grounds.

I contacted him, and it was the proverbial match made in heaven. We could easily exchange labs and courses. After a swap of pictures, he and his wife loved our house and vice versa. We even decided to trade pets. We had a Siamese cat named Bob, and they had an indeterminate breed dog named Ginger, neither of whom gave signs of being able to travel well (they had a cat too, but it was almost invisible. The only reason we knew it existed was the evidence it left in the cat box.).

And the trains! Oh, the trains! Santa Fe. Southern Pacific. BIG power. Mining roads. I salivated at the thought. Besides, I was a fourth-generation Westerner. Like going home. We signed the papers, made arrangements for a temporary housesitter until the Whitfords arrived, and then started to think about how we'd get there.

First thought, of course, by train. Maybe down to New Orleans, then over to El Paso. But then reality reared its ugly head. We'd need a vehicle down there, and there was all the JUNK required for a long stay. So there had to be an alternative.

You know how when you're younger, you have certain dreams and ambitions, and when you grow up, you say, "Thank GOD I didn't do that!" Confession time. I'd always had this idea of being a long-haul truck driver. It was partly the idea of "Route 66," and part the idea of being in command of a giant Peterbilt, parting the cars ahead like dolphins in front of a battleship. At one point early in my faculty years, I even toyed with the idea

165

of buying a gigantic Kenworth tractor, leasing it out to somebody for 9 months, then driving myself on the transcontinental run during the summer. Well, that never worked out. So, as a nice substitute for youthful dreams of 18-wheelers, how about instead a nice Dodge Dakota 4-wheel drive pickup, and we *drive* to Las Cruces?

We allotted a week for the trip, and decided it would partly be on the freeway, and partly on the original, two lane highways to see what the Real America looked like before the freeways. Bad idea. Some things best left to ignorance.

We took Interstate 95 down to New York, then the Jersey Turnpike, then headed west to pick up Interstate 81. This was a revelation. We didn't know it, but 81 was the Mother of all Truck Routes. Sometimes we were the only "four-wheeler" in sight. The CB craze was long over, but we had a little CB, hoping perhaps to pick up "Smokey" tips about potential speed traps. These would have been good to have, because it seemed like the average speed for the 18-wheelers was about 85, and if you were much slower you got the finger, the horn, and the scare of your life. The independent truckers got paid by the load, hence the faster you went, the more you netted. However, CB conversation had degenerated to the point that internet chat seems to have today; all foul mouthed, incoherent trolls. My recollection is a bit dim, but it sounded sort of like this; "Hey, you #&%$%^$, I got me beaver fever. Anybody know where there's a #*&&^% beaver palace that got some concrete blondes?" I won't bother to translate.

Pretty soon it was time for our first Truck Stop restaurant lunch. Folklore had it that truck stops were the last refuge of genuine country cooking, so we were actually looking forward to our first experience.

The initial surprise when we walked in was to see the rank and unashamed snobbery. Most of the counter seats and the majority of the booths had big signs; "Professional Drivers Only." The booths near the kitchen and bathroom entrances said, "Others," but the implication was clear. "Other"

166

meant "Those Who Should Not be Cluttering the Highways for Real Drivers."

Savoring an en route meal.

Then there was the food. The average meal was maybe 5,200 calories, partly because the mystery meat was deep fried in diesel oil. A lot of the food you could either eat or put directly in your truck's fuel tank because it had so much trans fat (I believe "trans" is actually short for "transmission").

After we waddled out of our first truck stop, being of a naturally generous nature, we thought that we had somehow stumbled onto a bad 'un. Unfortunately the next one wasn't much different. After a few of these, at the next meal time we decided to get off at a town exit and see if we could find an excellent small-town local restaurant like the ones that were becoming the norm in southern Rhode Island. The first time we tried this, exact location mercifully forgotten but somewhere in Tennessee, we discovered a type of restaurant that was unfamiliar to us; a "Family" restaurant.

Turns out that a Family restaurant is one that not only tolerates, but seems to welcome the worst kind of youthful behavior. Things like booger flicking, food up the nose stuffing, and fart contests. Positives? The food was dirt cheap, and probably not poisonous. It became a contest. When passing through long rural stretches of highway where truck stops were few and far between, we used to have competitions to see how hungry we could get before finally succumbing and following the signs to the next Family restaurant. I think we each gained about 10 pounds on our trip, and my fantasy of being a long-haul trucker died forever.

There were some wonderful and bizarre things along the way. We stopped in Memphis to pay homage to Elvis, of course. As a teen nerd in the '50s, I hated Elvis on general principle, because the girls all seemed to go ga-ga over his greaser image, and his success only made things worse. With the passage of time, I actually grew to like his music, so a stop at Graceland was not out of order. We met some true Elvis fans in the many lines we waited in, and they were charming if ununderstandable to me, although some churl had scrawled "He's dead-get a life" among the adoring messages written on the stone wall around the mansion.

A wonderful sentiment on a Graceland wall.

We got off the highway for a day-long sojourn through the hill country of Arkansas, and there we stumbled across a candidate for most unusual town name in America. Toad Suck, Arkansas. Really. It's an unincorporated area near the University of Central Arkansas.

After that, we elected to follow secondary roads through Lubbock, Texas, Alamogordo, New Mexico, and then down to Las Cruces. The countryside became starker and more dramatic, and before long we were forced to admit that we weren't in New England any more. The roadside attractions also became more folksy, featuring souvenir stores composed of acres of silver-painted statues of liberty, cowboys, skyscrapers, and other kitsch.

A bastion of good taste.

There were constant reminders that New Mexico was the birthplace of the atomic bomb. It was developed at Los Alamos in the northern part of the state, and first tested in the desolate *Jornada del Muerte* (journey of death) plain about 90 miles from Las Cruces. The closer we got to town, the more black humor examples of the incorporation of The Bomb into local folklore we saw, including the "Atomic Pest Control" company, that had a giant mutant mouse on its roof, and an alien leprechaun with antennae on his head on its billboard.

When you want really *powerful* rat killers.

We arrived as scheduled, found the Whitford's house (they were waiting for us to arrive before they left), got briefed on the household routine, met Ginger the dog, who immediately beseeched us for a walk (run), and briefly caught a glimpse of the invisible cat that we saw maybe four times in as many months. We had come "home."

Before the merger with the Burlington Northern Railroad.

Okay, the trains. Las Cruces is not a railroad town, per se, but is on what was a secondary line of the Santa Fe from El Paso, Texas to Albuquerque. You would occasionally see a Santa Fe through freight passing through town, but regular freight service to the town ended in 1988. Most of the rail "action" was within a couple of hours drive, but as I quickly discovered there was more railfan consciousness in Las Cruces than in any place I'd ever been.

After a couple of weeks, I saw a notice in the local paper about a meeting of the local model railroad club. They had a layout at the local fairgrounds. It was jaw-dropping; huge, and with an extraordinary level of craftsmanship. Most of the buildings and rolling stock were scratch built to museum standards. I was *clearly* out of my league.

At this first meeting I met a guy named Bill Morrison, who I came to worship. Bill was overweight, nearsighted, chainsmoked, and was probably the best miniature craftsman I ever met. His specialty was making scale model buildings, but the thing that was different about his buildings was that they were made the same way the "real" building was; joists, rafters, studs, headers, etc. I became a kind of apprentice to Bill over the next few months, and he gave me tips on where the good railfan spots were.

I had to get used to a different scale of distance than I was used to in Little Rhody. Most of the good rail sites were at least 40 miles from Las Cruces, which would have been "out of state" in Rhode Island. But the traffic was so light, and the roads so good that the concept of "pleasure driving" returned, and almost every weekend there was some kind of jaunt.

One of my first targets was the Southern Pacific Sunset Line main that came in from Tucson, Arizona to the west, went almost straight to Deming, New Mexico, then headed southeast to El Paso, Texas. This was heavy-duty freight railroading at its best; heavy mineral trains, and hot-shot double-stack container and trailer trains. Most of the engines you saw were lettered "SSW," which stood for "St. Louis Southwestern," a wholly owned subsidiary of the SP whose more familiar name was the "Cotton Belt." The

SSW symbol freight racing through Deming. Note coal tower in background.

downside of hunting trains on an isolated line like this was that in the days before railfans started carrying radio scanners, and most of the trains were unscheduled, it was a bit of luck if you were at a good spot at the same time that a train came through. This line was particularly interesting, because it ran through one of the only places on the SP's system where there were enough coal deposits to support coal-burning, rather than oil-burning steam locomotives. Most of them were pretty conventional looking, but when the SP did something different, they did it *really* different. In 1939 SP ordered a dozen million-pound AC-9 streamlined articulated locomotives, the only ones ever built. They operated through New Mexico until 1952, when they were converted to oil, and moved to an isolated SP line in northern California, where they served until retirement in 1956.

Our first major rail sidetrip was a visit to the enormous Santa Rita (Chino) copper mine, located in the center-west part of the state. There had been copper mining there since before the Spanish days, but the open-pit mine didn't start til 1909, when the Colorado mining entrepreneur Spencer Penrose opened it. Rail played an important part in the development of the mine and smelters around it.

To get to the mine, there's a quick way, and a colorful way. We took the latter. You first drive north up the freeway to one of New Mexico's many Chili Capitals of the World, in this case, Hatch.

At Hatch, you turn left and start driving on a two-line road where you passed another car every 15 minutes or so (try that in Rhode Island). You keep going until you come to the middle of nowhere. You know you've arrived, because right there in the charming ghost town of Nutt, New Mexico, there is the "Middle of Nowhere Bar and Café." The road to Nutt (Yes, that's its real name. It is named after Col Henry Clay Nutt) paralleled a Santa Fe branch line from Rincon in the Rio Grande Valley southwest toward Deming on the SP. We wanted to get in a little mountain driving, however, so we cut northwest from Nutt across the desert to the Black Range mountains, and then west.

The sign says it.

After a couple of hours of very pleasant driving, as we approached the small town of Hanover at an elevation of about 6,500 feet, on our left we saw the enormous mine. A huge old open-pit mine, like the Santa Rita, or the Bingham Canyon in Utah has the same effect on the viewer as the Grand Canyon; you are dumbfounded and can't really find words to describe it.

Southwestern locomotive at Hurley, New Mexico.

I knew something of the history of the mine, and mines in general and their toxic effects on the environment. Terrible. Shut them down. But then, what would I want to give up first to reduce my copper consumption? How about the truck? Lot of copper wire in a truck. How about electricity in the house? Those damned power lines coming to the house; copper. Clearly a dilemma, but one I was clueless to resolve, so I went back to Admirer of Human Enterprise mode, and the mine was clearly an achievement in that department.

The mine itself was no longer worked by electric railroads and the ore was concentrated, then hauled by truck to the mill town of Hurley, where there was a smelter and extractor plant that served the Santa Rita mine, and the nearby on-again-off-again Tyrone open pit mine. At Hurley, there was extensive railroad trackwork, and from the road, you could easily see locomotives and trains of the Southwestern Railroad. The Southwestern Railroad is a shortline cobbled together in 1990 from little-used Santa Fe

174

branches in western New Mexico.

The principle products of the smelter were yard-square, two-inch thick copper plates called "anodes," which weighed about 900 pounds (worth about $2,500 at today's price). These anodes were about 98% pure copper, insufficient for most industrial needs. So about 50 of them at a time were loaded onto flatcars, than hauled by Southwestern locomotives down to Deming, where they were switched over to the SP for transport to the huge Phelps Dodge refinery on the outskirts of El Paso (closed in 2007).

Reminder of bygone days.

The mine and the plants in Hurley have operated on an on-off basis since my visit, depending on the world price of copper. I understand everything is still pretty much in place, thus well worth a visit by the devoted railfan.

Our next sidetrip that had a railroad component did not, I must admit, have trains as its primary objective. I am of the last generation that has some personal acquaintance with the events of the early atomic age. My uncle serviced radar units on Tinian Island, where the *Enola Gay,* the B-29 that dropped the atomic bomb on Hiroshima was based. I have a couple of old photos of Hiroshima taken in 1917 by my grandfather when he came back from the mines of Korea. My meteorology course in college was taught by the meteorologist who had to give the final go to the world's first atomic bomb test in New Mexico. This interest led me eventually to teach an Honors college course on the atom bomb not long before my retirement. So, I wanted to visit the atomic museum at Los Alamos and if possible, the Trinity Site where the first bomb went off. By stroke of fortune, these attractions were not far from Albuquerque and Santa Fe, where there was also plenty of rail interest.

Twice a year, the Trinity atomic bomb test site is open to the public. We planned our trip north to Albuquerque to take advantage of the event. At Alamogordo, you formed a convoy with other cars, which then drove the 70 miles or so to the site in the middle of the *Jornada*. The first surprising thing was that without a chain link fence surrounding ground zero, you'd never know that there had been an enormous explosion there. They had trucked most of the radioactive soil away after the blast, and in 50 years, the desert had pretty much recovered.

There wasn't really much to see. There was a little hot dog trailer to refresh yourself, and near the entrance to the site was a huge piece of steel that looked like a length of giant sewer pipe with 10 inch thick walls. It was called "Jumbo" and was originally designed to contain the radioactive uranium if the bomb had been a dud. There was a guide with a Geiger counter who was happy to demonstrate that there was more radioactivity in people's old luminous watches than there was in the fused glass sand left over from the explosion.

"Fat Man" atomic bomb casing. This is not a replica, but one of the original set from which the Nagasaki bomb was made.

The centerpiece of the site was an actual original atomic bomb casing from the same batch that was used for the Nagasaki bomb. It was trucked down from Los Alamos on a flatbed trailer. I noticed a curious phenomenon. All of the visitors were strangely attracted to the bomb on its trailer, including myself. And everyone, including myself, felt compelled to touch it. It is hard to describe, but it felt *evil*. I'm not sure that I know exactly what that means, but it had an ominous presence, and once having touched it, people didn't linger, even though it was just an empty shell.

The only permanent feature on the site was a modest stone obelisk, with a bronze plaque identifying the location as the Trinity site. This proved to be a favored location for visitor's snapshots. I noticed that quite a few visitors were Japanese, which was, I suppose, not surprising considering the importance of The Bomb in their country's history. However, in a bizarre note, when the Japanese visitors posed in front of the monument they struck silly poses and mugged for the cameras, just like Boston Red Sox fans do in front of the Ted Williams statue in Boston. Nervousness? I had no explanation and felt too awkward to ask.

Where the Trinity bomb was assembled.

There was another grotesque note to the site. A few miles away from ground zero, the ranch house of the McDonald ranch on which the site was located had been preserved. The house had been commandeered by the army for the final assembly of the bomb initiator. The building was still there and you could wander through it. This was the place where the most powerful weapon the world had ever known had been put together, but the only visible sign was a conspicuous one outside the building warning visitors to "Beware of Snakes."

We stopped for a few hours at the wonderful Bosque del Apache National Wildlife Refuge near Soccoro, then went straight on to Santa Fe. Curiously, neither the communities of Atchison, Topeka, nor Santa Fe are on the original route of the Atchison, Topeka, and Santa Fe Railroad.

For rail enthusiasts, Santa Fe is a jumping-off point, rather than a major destination. The Santa Fe Railroad had a branch from Lamy, on the main line, to Santa Fe, but it had been abandoned at about the time of our visit. However, a consortium of local businesses bought the branch, and renamed it the Santa Fe Southern. They were primarily running freight, but had recently started a tourist passenger operation. They had some nicely painted low-hood GP-7s, and a fetching caboose. Alas, the line closed in 2014.

The *real* reason to go to Santa Fe is not the dozens of art galleries and the opera house, but the fact that it is the southern gateway to two of the most scenic train rides in the United States, the Cumbres and Toltec,

Santa Fe, New Mexico train station.

and the Durango and Silverton. They are today geographically and administratively separated, but they were at one time the southern and northern legs of the Denver and Rio Grande Railroad's narrow gauge San Juan Extension that ran between Silverton and Santa Fe, via Durango, Chama, and Antonito, Colorado.

We didn't have a chance to take either of these runs, but on a previous transcontinental trip, I made a stopover to ride the Durango and Silverton line. Yes, it is touristy, but the line, through the cañyon of the Rio de las Animas is stunning, and even a bit scary, because the ledge the tracks are laid on is cut out of a cliff, and there is barely enough width for the train. A huge bonus is the fact that the passenger trains are still drawn by beautifully maintained 2-8-2 steam locomotives.

The semester passed all too quickly. We bid a tearful farewell to Ginger the dog, and set out on a nightmarish return to Rhode Island. We were in a hurry to get back home (which is always a mistake on a long trip), and it was December. The Family restaurants were even more dismal than we remembered, and there was a raging snowstorm on the Massachusetts Turnpike when we crossed the Berkshires, and we slip-slid most of the way home.

179

On our return to our house in Rhode Island, the first thing our beloved cat, Bob, did when Marjorie reached down to pet him was bite her hand. Take THAT for abandoning me for a year! Things soon settled down, and we began to look forward to a long stretch of peaceful time in our home; maybe get back to model railroading instead of railfanning. Boy, did that turn out to be a wish that didn't come true.

Chapter 13

The 1:30 to Tenom

We hadn't been back from New Mexico for long before I realized that I was still eligible for a sabbatical, but hadn't yet taken one. So I started looking around for places to go where I might be able to do something a little different in teaching or research, but still might have a chance to increase my train experience inventory. I had received a Fulbright fellowship in 1981, and idly started browsing through the then-current Fulbright brochure. I discovered that, A) I was eligible to receive a second Fulbright, and B) There was an opportunity listed that practically had my name written on it (as I look back on my academic career, it is strange how many things apparently had my name written on them).

This time around, however, I was married and wasn't really sure how Marjorie would feel about this particular opportunity. It would be a major inconvenience for her. She would have to find somebody to cover her practice for a year, and find alternatives for all her current patients. So it was with some trepidation that I went home that night and asked, non-committally, "Say, how'd you like to spend a year in Borneo?" She thought about it for a few seconds, and replied, "How many suitcases could I bring?" I knew then that I had married the right woman.

Fulbright opportunities to teach American History at Oxford had many, many applicants, but I had a feeling that if I applied for this particular one, I wouldn't have much competition. It seems that the Ministry of Education of His Majesty, Sultan Haji Hassanal Bolkiah Mu'izzaddin Waddaulah, Sultan and Yang Di-Pertuan of Brunei Darussalam, at the time the world's richest man, and one of the world's few absolute monarchs, wanted an

American Fulbright scholar to come over and help set up a program to teach college science teachers how to teach in their newly established university, Universiti Brunei Darusalaam. Piece of cake, right up my alley. I applied, and duly received word that I had been accepted for the fall of 1995.

When I saw the terms, I thought I'd died and gone to heaven. My university would pay me half my regular salary, the U.S. State Department, which ran the Fulbright program, paid the other half, their Ministry of Education would pay airfare (business class) for Marjorie and me out and back, plus a a trip home at Christmas. They'd also provide a free apartment with room service in a hotel-apartment, and a car. Plus, the State Department would pick up the tab for travel if I wanted to give guest lectures anywhere in Southeast Asia.

This generosity was because this was considered a "hardship post." Heck, I don't know why. Brunei was almost right on the equator. The temperature didn't vary more than a degree or so, day or night, summer or winter, from 96°. Humidity was a pretty constant 95%. When we walked to town, we had to navigate around the 8 foot monitor lizard, and a troop of crab-eating macaque monkeys, whose very irritable male leader had canine teeth about three inches long that he liked to flash at you. You had to have malaria shots, and one day I found a banded krait, one of the deadliest snakes in the world, resting in the shade of my car, the interior of which would go to about 170° at noon. Other than that, it was a great place.

I had initially thought that it was foolish of the Bruneian government to spend all that money for a Fulbright visitor, until I found out the going rate for educational consultants from Britain or Australia to Brunei. About a thousand dollars a *day* plus expenses. So Fulbrighters were really a bargain.

As part of my advance research, I looked up what the railroad situation would be. There had been many short logging and mining railroads built over the years in Borneo, the island on which the tiny country of Brunei was located. However, as soon as the trees or the ore were gone, the forest reclaimed the railroads and left not a trace, usually within five years or so of abandonment. Despite that, I thought that if I hunted hard enough and took enough trips, I might be able to find some vestiges of some of the old logging or mining lines. I had heard that there was a still-operating remnant of the North Borneo Railway, built in 1898 by the Brits in nearby Sabah, a section of Borneo that administratively was a state of the country of Malaysia, so that was a must visit. In nearby countries, I anticipated being able to find quite a few railroads. Hong Kong had many rail connections to mainland China. Peninsular Malaysia had a long line that connected to Singapore in the south and Thailand in the north; from there it was (maybe) possible to take a train into old Burma (Myanmar). Vietnam was known to have a rail link from north to south, but was still closed to American visitors. So, not like Switzerland but not a total vacuum, either.

We made arrangements for a housesitter for a year, bad farewell to family and friends, and in August of 1995, set out on our halfway-around-the-world trip. There had been paperwork delays, and by the time we were cleared to make our air reservations, we found that all the business class seats on our transpacific flight were gone, and the only coach seats left were in the last row before the coach smoking section. Collectively, we have forgotten that smoking used to be allowed on airplanes, but it was the norm on international flights in the mid-'90s. An anonymous wag once said, "Having a smoking section on an airplane is like having a peeing section in a swimming pool." People who smoke typically light up when they're stressed, flying is stressful, so sitting right in front of the smoking section was like being in the fire department's training house for fire rescues. Other than that, the flight was great. Back then, international coach was almost like domestic business class is today. Sigh.

We changed flights in Tokyo, and our next stop was Hong Kong. The new Hong Kong airport had not yet opened, and we flew the Runway 13 approach into the old Kai Tak airport. This was known among airline pilots as the most challenging major airport runway in the world. For passengers nervous about flying, it was known as the "Kai Tak Heart Attack." Your 747 pilot approached at a stunningly low altitude right over the city, taking aim at a huge checkerboard sign posted on a hill. When he judged that he was at the right point, he'd make a 30 degree right bank at an altitude of only about 1,000 feet, then drop like a rock to make the end of the runway, which was marginally long enough for a 747, with the harbor on each end. On the north side of the runway and only about 200 feet away, was a line of 6 story apartment blocks. You could almost see what folks were having for dinner through their windows. Hmmm. Kung Pao chicken. Looks pretty good. The airlines used only their best and most experienced pilots for Kai Tak (if you don't like to fly, and want to scare yourself to death, look up "Kai Tak landings" on YouTube.).

We had been booked in the Peninsula Hong Kong Hotel, which was not

Kowloon-New Territories train. These were 18 cars long, and they ran at 15 minute intervals.

hard to take, and I immediately checked out the train scene. Great Britain would not turn Hong Kong over to the People's Republic of China until 1997, so it was still difficult to get into China proper from Hong Kong without a lot of time-consuming formalities. Fortunately, the Hong Kong Railway Museum was located on the old Kowloon-Canton railway in the northern part of the New Territories, close to the China border. We could get to the museum by using one of the electric interurban railways that paralleled the main line.

In addition to its colorful double-decker streetcars and Peak Tram, Hong Kong has a network of modern interurban railroads connecting the three districts; Hong Kong Island, Kowloon on the mainland, and New Territories. The Peninsula was in Kowloon, reasonably close to the train station, but many of the attractions were on Hong Kong Island, which was reachable on one of the greatest ferryboat rides in the world, the Star Ferry.

Star Ferry, Hong Kong to Kowloon.

Hong Kong was wonderful for strolling and looking at the often weird signs. When Asian sentences are translated into English, the results are sometimes odd or startling. The "Long Full" restaurant sort of made sense, but the "Perfect Wound Competition Motors" company that made racing accessories for Honda cars was a head scratcher

From Hong Kong it was a short hop to our next stopping place, Singapore. The city-state was in the headlines the year before because a young American named Michael Fay had

That always happens to me after a big meal.

been caned with a lash for vandalizing cars. As vandalizing cars was not on our agenda we were not overly concerned, but quickly discovered that Singapore was a lovely city where everything appeared to work. There was also a *lot* of money that appeared to be floating around. We were assigned to the Mandarin Oriental Hotel, only a short walk from the Long Bar at the Raffles Hotel where we were able to sample the original Singapore Sling (if there are any graduate students reading this; these opportunities are why you work very, very hard in graduate school).

We had to stay about a week in Singapore while final details were arranged for our trip to Brunei on Royal Brunei Airlines. It was a brief flight into the very modern international airport (The Sultan was a pilot, and used his main private plane, a Boeing 747-400, to practice takeoffs and landings at the airport every Monday). We were picked up by a driver from the American Embassy and taken to our hotel-apartment close to town. On the way in, I was surprised. I'd heard much about the legendary wealth of the place, but as I looked around, it appeared like a typical riverbank

186

tropical town I'd seen a dozen times in the Philippines. Appearances can be deceiving.

What then followed was a year that was so bizarre for an average, middle-class American couple that it almost defies description. Hell, it *does* defy description. After we were there for a while, Marjorie got a job working for the royal family in a medical capacity, which gave her access to places and circumstances that I would love to talk about, but can't, due to patient confidentiality concerns. Most of these strange happenings didn't have anything to do with trains, so will have to wait for another book, but I'll give you a taste.

I had a private pilot's licence by now and I found that there was a flying club based at the airport that owned an aircraft I was qualified to fly. Most of the members were professional pilots, who worked either for the royal family or Royal Brunei Airlines, but just liked to fly little planes for fun. In the course of "hangar talk," I asked the 747 guys how they maintained flight proficiency in the big plane, because the family only used it a few times a month. They said that the Sultan let them use the 747 for personal errands so they could keep current. One of the pilots had a Harley-Davidson motorcycle, and as you might imagine, parts were hard to come by in Brunei, so they would regularly bop over to Singapore to have some of that great Singapore mei fun for lunch and pick up a couple of spark plugs. On the Sultan's dime.

It was public knowledge that the Sultan loved cars, and owned over 200 Ferraris. That was puzzling. Brunei's roads were crowded, and generally not built to modern standards. So where do you drive your Ferrari? When I was taking my check flight in the little Cessna 172, the check pilot directed me to a forested area that was off the beaten path to anywhere. There below me, was a private motor racing course, where one could practice 4-wheel drifts in your TestaRossa. One does get tired of driving, and after all the concentration that racing requires, a nice horseback ride would clear one's head. For His Majesty, this was easy. He had 200 polo ponies, and the best part was that he could take his favorites with him when he traveled, because his 747 had a stable in the baggage compartment! Oh, by the way, Michael Jackson provided the entertainment for His Majesty's 50th birthday party, and Whitney Houston was the wedding singer for a daughter.

Perhaps the most educational part of this year for me, was that Brunei was a Muslim country, and like most Americans, I knew almost nothing about Islam and I discovered that what I thought I knew was mostly wrong. As I was teaching in a strongly Islamic context, I felt that I had to learn something about it to be an effective teacher, and eventually ended up writing a little guidebook to Islam and Islamic science for non-Muslim teachers that was published by the University.

I could find mention of only two railroads in Brunei. One was built to connect the Brooketon Colliery, a major source of energy export in the '20s and before, to the deepwater port of Muara. It was only a couple of miles long, had wooden rails, and shut down in 1924.

The other had even less information about it, and none in any written records. In asking around, I heard stories about a short railroad that had been built to transport workers from one Shell jobsite to another on one of the northwest coast towns, possibly Limut. I never did find any physical traces of it so can't be sure it existed.

The chances of finding remains of an old logging railroad were better. Brunei had "struck it rich" with offshore natural gas deposits in 1974, and not long after, developed a strong environmental consciousness--because it could afford to. I mentioned earlier that we passed a huge monitor lizard daily on our walk to town. In most other parts of SE Asia that lizard would have been somebody's lunch, because monitor lizards are tasty and good nutrition. In Brunei, people didn't forage any more because they could afford expensive Australian beef, and besides, in two generations, the people of Brunei essentially went from forest people to urbanites and they didn't want to have anything to do with the idea of returning to the forest for anything.

In railroad terms, this meant that logging came to a *screeching* halt, with the result that you could find abandoned log dumps, mills, and sharp forest edges as soon as you got a few miles away from the capitol city. On one trip with the Brunei Nature Society, I hit pay dirt; the abandoned tracks of what looked to be a 24" gauge logging line. Unfortunately, there was no equipment to be seen. That was the only evidence of a railroad I ever found in Brunei.

We made several trips to Sarawak, the southernmost state of Malaysia on Borneo. The objective of these trips was not railfanning, because other than a few puzzling references to railroads in old journals we had no concrete evidence that there had ever been railroads there. Rather, Sarawak was a place where you could have

Abandoned logging road. In back of the author is virgin forest. In almost any other part of SE Asia, this would have been cut down years ago.

a *Heart of Darkness/Apocalypse Now* adventure, traveling upriver in dugout canoes to visit the longhouses of tribes who had, only a generation ago, been headhunters. With our jumping off place in Kuching, the delightful capital city which had one of the two cat museums in the world ("Kuching" means "cat"), we visited an Iban tribe longhouse. We arranged this trip through a friend in Brunei who was an expatriate Iban. Today we understand that you can now buy packaged tourist visits to longhouses, but then it was still a bit of an adventure, not least because when we got to the longhouse, we discovered hanging in a basket from the ceiling, a half dozen blackened human skulls, undoubtedly from previous visitors who hadn't paid for their lunch. Needless to say we were thenceforth on our *best*

Low tippers.

behavior. We never did ride any trains in Sarawak, but while wandering around in a small village near the Mulu Caves, I found the remains of a little homemade locomotive. I'm guessing it had something to do with logging, because mining railroad operations tend not to use internal combustion engines.

The other Malaysian state in Borneo, Sabah, was quite a different story. It had the North Borneo Railway, started by British interests to carry tobacco, a new crop grown in the interior to the port city of Weston. It was later extended to the capitol city, what is now called Kota Kinabalu. There was fierce fighting in this area during World War II, and the line was almost completely destroyed. After the war, the line was slowly rebuilt, mostly by Australians, but its primary mission was now to haul varied agricultural products and logs to port. When we visited, there was regular passenger train service, and the vast majority of the passengers were locals.

At the time of our visit, there was very little tourism in Borneo. Marjorie and I were in a group of only six Americans living in Brunei, although there were quite a few Brits and 'Strines (Australians). When we

Logging "engine" at Mulu, Sarawak.

190

traveled in the back country, if we did see westerners, they were usually there on business and they were almost never Americans. So we were extremely conspicuous, and very aware of the fact that we were, even in an informal way, representing the US.

When we visited Sabah, we went primarily to ride the North British Railway, which at the time of our visit was called the Sabah State Railway. The line was built by the Brits to serve inland agricultural areas, destroyed by the Japanese during WWII, then rebuilt after the war with massive US aid. However, as the later monstrous wave of tourism suggested, it was a fabulous place to visit if you were interested in nature. Some of the best diving in the world, the tallest mountain in Borneo (13,000 feet), orangutans, the largest flower in the world (*Rafflesia*), giant pythons (a 26 foot one ate a plantation worker during our visit); what's not to like?

The train to Tenom. Japanese equipment, but note the American style knuckle coupler.

We planned to take the train from Kota Kinabalu, the capitol, to the end of the line in the interior at Tenom. We boarded the train in early afternoon. It was not impressive to look at; three non-airconditioned coaches with wooden bench seats, and a "baggage" car. Sometimes there's a flat car, and you can sit on it in the open air. It was pulled by an old Japanese diesel. The run to the first major junction town, Beaufort, ran through flat tropical agricultural land and was, I admit, a tad boring. But at Beaufort, the line to Tenom branched and headed east, straight to the Crocker mountain range, and the Padas River Gorge. Today, this river is a white-water rafting destination. Then, it was just a place that could kill you, as landslides regularly dumped on the tracks, or the tracks (and a train) slid off into the river because the ground was so waterlogged. The locals didn't seem to be bothered by this, so we decided not to be bothered either.

One of the main reasons the native forest is just about gone from SE Asia.

Tropical gorges tend not to be, on close inspection, as spectacular as arid land canyons, because they're covered by trees, some of which reached almost 300 feet in Sabah. This vegetative cover softens the contours of the

192

land. The huge first-growth tropical trees grow very slowly, because the soil is generally thin and poor, but when they're cut, the second-and-+third growth grasses, vines and shrubs fill in very quickly. The railroad didn't use herbicides or fire to keep its right of way clear, so the tracks were covered with a foot or two of vegetative growth that blended perfectly with the surrounding landscape. This was rather disconcerting when you realized the engineer couldn't actually see any rails in front of him. When you are boogieing through swampland, this might be considered a bit of a hazard to timid souls, but by then we had adapted the "bahala na" attitude of our Filipino friends, which meant, loosely, "whatever will be, will be." Today, in addition to the regular train still operated by the SSR, a local luxury resort hotel operates a steam powered tourist train over part of the route.

As I did the research for this book, I used a variety of Web sources, including Google Earth. It struck me, as I looked at places I had visited only 20 years ago, that if I returned today they would be almost unrecognizable to me. The capitol city of Brunei, Bandar Seri Begawan, which was just a small backwater tropical rivermouth city with a scattering of villages on stilts that hadn't changed in a hundred years had its population quintuple since we were there. The nature of tourism has also changed dramatically. In the "exotic" places we visited in SE Asia, we were usually one of only a few Western visitors and typically the only Americans.

However, in 1996, through the American Embassy in Brunei, a visit was arranged for me to have some informal and unofficial talks with the department of education in Vietnam, and Marjorie accompanied me. We were thus among the first American non-military "tourists" in Vietnam since the war. Unfortunately, we didn't have time to take the train from Hanoi to Ho Chi Minh City. Now, "adventure travel" has been commercialized and sanitized; the term produces 3,600,000 hits on Google, and Vietnam has about 400,000 American visitors a year. So, all in all, I think we were there at the right time.

Our final SE Asian trip had a variety of objectives. One of my colleagues at the university had strongly recommended that we visit Penang, in Peninsular Malaysia, where there was a Buddhist snake temple. And Marjorie had a childhood dream of... riding an elephant. Now, I suppose there are a lot of places where you can hitch a ride on Jumbo, but Thailand had banned logging in protected areas in 1989, and all of a sudden, about 3,000 logging elephants went on unemployment. Some Thai genius figured that crazy Western tourists might pay good money to ride an elephant, and the former training centers for elephants in northern Thailand got turned into elephant Disneylands. At the time of our visit, though, they were pretty primitive, just you, a mahout, a rocky crooked trail, and an elephant. And the best part was that you could get there by train.

I'm fibbing a bit here. What I'm about to describe occurred over several separate trips, but I'm condensing a little to save space. In all cases, we started at the 1930's built art deco train station in Singapore. A few hours later, you're in the capitol city of Malaysia, Kuala Lumpur, which has a wonderful Victorian train station, not far from the Petronas towers. From there, it is only a couple of hour's ride to Penang on the west coast of the peninsula. Penang is the home of one of the world's greatest unheralded cuisines, *Nyonya,* which is a combination of Chinese and Indonesian-spicy. Lord, I'm getting hungry just thinking about it.

The trains on the Malaysian State Railways were nothing to write home about. Most of the equipment was the ubiquitous Kawasaki or Hitachi Japanese rolling stock found all over SE Asia. Comfortable but boring. In Penang, on my colleague's recommendation, we visited the Fu Ling Gong Buddhist snake temple. Appeared to be your basic Buddhist temple, but for some reason there were cut-off tree branches all over the place, and sure enough, there were snakes slithering all through the branches. All kinds of snakes. I recognized a lot of your basic constrictors, but there were also some Asian pit vipers, related to our rattlesnakes. Fascinating.

Pretty soon this guy came up to me–he didn't look much like a monk–and I noticed he had some pit vipers draped over his shoulders. He smiled broadly, and said to me in Malay, "Anda ingin memegang ular boleh membawa maut?" I didn't have the slightest idea what he was saying, but in Asia it is impolite to refuse, and I was trying to learn Malay so I said, "Memang!" which means, "Naturally! Of course." So his smile got bigger and he draped the snakes over *my* shoulders and head. What he had asked was, "Would you like me to put the snakes on you?" Marjorie took a picture of me, and I admit I didn't look

"Sure, I'd LOVE to pet a deadly viper!"

heroic. After I started breathing again, I sort of figured that maybe the snakes had been drugged, or had their fangs removed. My monk must have read my mind, because he smiled again, put one of the vipers on the floor, pulled a mouse out of a cage, and deposited it in front of the snake. Pow! Dead mouse. I made a ten buck donation to the temple. How often can you have a near-death experience and get your picture taken for only ten dollars?

I just looked up the Fu Ling Gong snake temple on Trip Adviser. They're still in business, but they don't say anything about visitors holding snakes, or even getting close to snakes. They must have lost a couple of customers.

It was on the next leg of the trip that I have the only regret about all our travels in SE Asia. The same company that runs the Venice Simplon Orient Express in Europe ran a luxury train called the Eastern and Oriental

195

Express between Singapore and Bangkok. We *could* have afforded it (barely), but instead we were prudent. As an alternative, we took the regular Malaysian State Railways overnight train. There was nothing wrong with it, but luxury it was not.

Bangkok was overwhelming. Unbelievable traffic. Noise. Confusion. Gorgeous temples. Exquisite food. We stayed a couple of days, then it was another overnight train to Chaing Mai in the north. Chaing Mai was a foothill city with many outdoor bazaars and food stall areas. I thought I had pushed my food and drink limits in Vietnam with *pinyin,* an aperitif drink made of cobra steeped in rice wine, but Chaing Mai presented a number of challenges, including steamed tadpoles served with a fermented fish sauce. Of course, there were also many delightful street dishes that could be eaten with relish by the timid.

We soon found out how to get to an elephant camp, and there were elephants everywhere, along with tourists, almost all Brits or 'Strines. Conditions were pretty basic. The proprietor looked us over, guessing our weight, I suppose, then assigned us to a mahout and Horton.

We first had to get into the howdah, or saddle. To do that, we climbed up a rickety stepladder arrangement, and at that point we discovered to our distress, that elephants are freakin' *tall*. This was before the lawyers discovered greenhorn elephant riding, and the howdah was just a wooden bench that, we supposed, one could easily bounce out of. Now, they have bars like roller coasters.

We started out in an arena-like ring, and we could see an undeveloped, rough trail leading off into the forest. The mahout looked back at us, we figured for a "go" signal. We nodded, he tapped Horton with his stick, and the goddam thing took off like an F-18 off the deck of the *USS Enterprise*. We weren't at all prepared for this. When I thought of "elephant ride," I was visualizing a gentle, rolling stroll, not a hell-for-leather gallop.

The trail was very irregular, and in a couple of places crossed an elephant belly-deep stream. Babar just plunged forward, creating waves big enough to surf on. After about 15 minutes of pure, unadulterated terror, mahout put on the brakes, the elephant stopped, and mahout got off. What?!? He then motioned that I was to get out of the howdah, and slide into the driver's position on the elephant's head. Marjorie had a frozen rictus on her face that was either joy or horror; I couldn't tell. I then assumed that as part of the price of the ride, I got the privilege of driving the elephant for a while. By sign language, I more-or-less learned the motions for "go," "left or right," and "stop." However, when I looked up to check if it was okay to proceed, the mahout had disappeared. Okay, I guess that meant I got the upcheck for my first solo flight.

Attempting to give a convincing impression that I know what I'm doing.

I now suspect that no matter what I signaled to the elephant, he was going to do what he usually did. If I suddenly got a yen to boogie off to Cambodia, Horton was just going to stay on the trail. However, he did respond pretty well to "stop" and "go". The trail described a kind of semicircle at that point, and after we had gone about a half mile, mahout appeared again. He'd just taken a short cut over the top of a hill.

It was a huge amount of fun, but I guess Marjorie got elephant riding out of her system, because I never heard her express a desire for an elephant ride again.

Mae Klong River train.

We returned to Bangkok for another, considerably more somber train side trip. The highly fictionalized David Lean movie "Bridge on the River Kwai" was loosely based on the construction of a bridge during WWII by Allied prisoners of war over the Mae Klong river at a town named Kanchanaburi, as part of a railroad built by the invading Japanese to go through Burma, in support of their intended eventual invasion of India. The bridge still exists, although heavily rebuilt. At Kanchanaburi, there is an Allied cemetery and museum devoted to the thousands of men who died building the railroad from that point through Burma. There is a special train that leaves from Bangkok that

198

allows time in Kanchanaburi, then crosses the bridge and travels along the river, at one point passing over the creaking (and somewhat terrifying) Wang Pho viaduct. This is, however, more a trip of reflection rather than scenery, as you recall the 16,000 Allied POW's who died constructing the railway.

We finished our year in South East Asia in the Spring of 1996. When we returned to Rhode Island, we realized we would never be the same again. And that wasn't necessarily a bad thing.

Chapter 14

I'm a Lumberjack and I'm Okay[2]

C anada is deceptive. Canadian cities (except those east of Montreal) sort of look like American cities. Canadian trains sort of look like American trains. Canadians sort of talk like Americans (except they say "aboot" instead of "about," unless they're from Quebec, in which case they say "sur"). However, if you are an American in Canada for more than a short, casual visit, you quickly learn that in many things, Canadians don't look at the world the same way Americans do. And one of the best ways to discover this is on an extended train trip.

Some of the great rail routes of the world are in Canada and may still be traveled. Unfortunately, some of the best are now defunct, or rerouted to more efficient, but less scenic lines. After Marjorie and I returned from Brunei, and got resettled into Rhode Island (a not inconsiderable task), we began to expand our rail horizons to the north.

There several ways to access Canada by rail from New England, but the main way starts from New York City. The surviving train north from there is called the *Adirondack*, and it follows the Hudson River to Albany, using the old New York Central water-level route, then continues north to Montreal on the banks of Lake Champlain using the old Delaware and Hudson Saratoga Division tracks. On one of our *Adirondack* trips in 2002, I stepped off the train at Albany for a photo break, and lucked out with two Amtrak oddities in one picture. The *Adirondack* at the time had a specially

---

[2] For those of you too young to remember the Monty Python TV show, this is a line from a bawdy little ditty called "The Lumberjack Song" © Terry Jones, Michael Palin, and Fred Tomlinson.

painted baggage car, with a mural-like mountain scene on each side. Alas, this service ended in 2003. On the other track was the sole survivor of Amtrak's RTL-II Rohr turboliner trains used in New York service. It was removed from service not long after our trip

The D & H had a very long and checkered history and is remembered by railfans today mostly because of its locomotives; during the steam era it pioneered a number of developments, like high boiler pressure and roller bearings. It also bought a set of the

Turboliner at Albany.

beautiful Alco PA diesel locomotives in the 1970s from the Santa Fe. I was lucky enough to catch a picture of one that was temporarily in Boston for service. *I* remembered the D & H because when I was a freshman at Rennsselaer in Troy, NY in 1959, I used to hitch rides on D & H freights from Troy to Albany, where the cool jazz clubs were (the drinking age in NY was 18 at the time). I'm pretty sure I actually rode a D & H train at least once. In my photo collection, I found an old (and not very good) picture of some D & H locomotives going past a small country station. I had an RPI girlfriend who lived with her parents in Watervliet, the first small country D & H station to the north of Albany. I'm guessing I bought a ticket.

Marjorie and I made several trips to Canada starting on this route. It is quite beautiful, in a quiet way, and the section along the Hudson is very reminiscent of the Rhine river. I'm not the only one to have made this observation; there are several towns along the way named "Rhine-"

201

something. When the line bends over to Lake Champlain, for much of the run you get better views of the lake than from any highway.

The jumping-off point for most long Canadian train trips is Montreal's *Gare Central* railroad station. This is an art-deco structure built in 1943. It has a very European feeling; much of the life of the city revolves around the train station. Above the station is one of the city's best hotels, the Fairmont The Queen Elizabeth. There is a private elevator that goes from the arrival hall of the station directly to the hotel. Very posh. Among the former attractions of the hotel was the quaintly (and some would say unfortunately) named upscale restaurant called "The Beaver Club." On our visit, they did not serve beaver. Montreal is a fabulous destination city, and whether it is an end point, or the starting point of a longer journey it is well worth as much time as you have to spend.

One December in the '00s, we decided to spend Christmas in Quebec City, about a three hour train ride from Montreal. The current operator of most Canadian rail service, VIA Rail, operates a corridor service between Quebec City, Montreal, Toronto, and Windsor, Ontario, that is much like the American Northeast Corridor, but it is not electrified. The weather in Quebec City in December is, ah, not for beach lovers. The average temperature is about 19o F, and there's a 66% chance that snow will fall on any given day. So we prepared by bringing enough winter clothing for the Russian Army during the invasion of Finland in 1939.

The run follows the St. Lawrence River for much of the way, and is pretty, but unremarkable until you approach the city. The dedicated railfan must instantly become alert, and be sure to sit on the right side of the train. A few miles outside the city, you can catch glimpses of one of the most remarkable bridges in the railroad world, the ill-fated Quebec Bridge.

Unlike the great Firth of Forth bridge mentioned in Chapter 10, the Quebec Bridge was not built to handle heavy rail traffic. It was built to *promote* heavy rail traffic between Quebec City and American markets to the south across the St. Lawrence River and the Maritime provinces to the east. It took many years of often crooked politics to secure the government funding to start the project and construction began in 1903. It was planned to be a single span cantilever bridge, the longest in the world. As construction proceeded it quickly became apparent that there were some severe design flaws; the bridge was much too heavy for its construction. On 29 August 1907, the bridge collapsed into the St. Lawrence carrying 75 workers to their doom. After a board of inquiry concluded that there had been gross negligence in the supervision of design and construction, the bridge's chief consulting engineer, Theodore Cooper, retired from the profession.

After much redesign and regrouping, construction started again. However, on September 11, 1916, as a new center span was being lifted into position, a lifting jack failed, and for the second time, part of the bridge collapsed into the river, killing another 11 workers. The third time was a charm, the bridge went into service in 1919, and has lived a productive and uneventful life ever since. It remains as the longest single span railroad cantilever bridge in the world.

The main train station in Quebec City is a delightful old structure built in 1915 to resemble a French palace. In fact, it's called the *Gare du Palais.* From there, it is a short distance to the old town. We stayed at a B & B in the old quarter, and in the course of one of our early strolls, we discovered a little jewel of a railroad surprise.

Quebec City is built above the banks of the St. Lawrence river, and a line of steep cliffs separates the plateau on which the main part of the city is located from the banks of the river. It was on part of this plateau that in 1759 Generals de Montcalm and Wolfe duked it out in the 30 minute Battle of the Plains of Abraham, that gave control of Canada to Great Britain in 1760. Much of the old port survives today, and one reaches it by means of a funicular railroad that starts at the upper end at the magnificent Le Château Frontenac hotel that is today run by the Fairmont chain. It is one of the two funiculars in Canada. Unfortunately, the cable on the funicular had broken in 1996 with fatal consequences for a British passenger. Needless to say, this fact was not to be found on the promotional material for the funicular but by this time, we had ridden on so many questionable means of transportation, I don't think it would have bothered us had we known. We had Christmas dinner at the Frontenac, and sat next to a rather famous TV cop known for roughing up suspects. Seemed pleasant enough to us.

About the same time period, we planned a transcontinental loop trip by train for summer. Up to Montreal, a connector train to Toronto, then VIA RAIL's *Canadian* to Vancouver. From there, a variously-named Amtrak train to Seattle, the *Empire Builder* to Chicago, the *Capitol Limited* to DC, then the Corridor back to Kingston. This would be a long trip; about 3 weeks with stops along the way, and be most unusual for us, in that it would be pure vacation.

Today, there are two major Canadian railroad companies; Canadian Pacific (CP), and Canadian National (CN), and two main transcontinental routes. The CP was the first one, completed in 1885 after about 10 years of work. Like the major American railroad lines, its history was replete with political chicanery, bribery, scandal, abuse of the labor force, and enormous difficulty in construction. The chief stimulus for building it was a requirement by British Columbia that a railroad be built to carry its products to the east as a condition for joining the Canadian confederation.

The CN had a more complex corporate history, and was more directly a product of government action than the CP. It also followed a more northern

204

transcontinental route once it became clear that agriculture was a viable proposition in the more northerly parts of the prairie states of Alberta, Saskatchewan, and Manitoba.

Both railroads operated competing transcontinental passenger trains, and in 1955, both modernized with the latest streamlined equipment. At this time the CN's premier train was called the *Super Continental*, which lacked a certain pizzaz, but the CP called its train simply the *Canadian* (or *Canadien,* depending on what part of Canada you were in). The *Canadian* was by far the classier train, being composed of stainless steel Budd equipment like the *California Zephyr*, or the *Sunset Limited*.

The CP route was the more spectacular of the two, as the CP had taken the shorter and what was thought at the time to be the only practical route through the Selkirk Range in British Columbia via Rogers and Kicking Horse Passes.

In the 1970s, Canada experienced the same reduction and consolidation of passenger train services as the US had earlier resulting in the formation of Amtrak. Canada's government-sponsored repository of the passenger train was called "Via Rail Canada," which was started in 1978. Shortly after, the *Super Continental* got the axe, leaving only the *Canadian* on the transcon run. Adding insult to injury, in 1990, the route of the *Canadian* was changed from the spectacular original CP route to the more northerly, and less interesting CN route. This change was puzzling, because it meant a loss of passenger train service to Regina, the capital of Saskatchewan, and Calgary, a near-million sized and very rich city. There have been suggestions that this move, like most others connected with Canadian railroads, was not based on economics but politics.

I had taken the *Canadian* cross country in 1970 from Rhode Island to Seattle. As I was preparing this chapter, I found an old picture of the observation car that had somehow been misplaced as I worked on earlier chapters. It suggested that both the train and the route were just as

The Canadian, 1970.

The Canadian, 2002.

gorgeous then as they were later.

Back to 2002. At this time, the *Canadian* originated in Toronto, rather than Montreal, so we had to take a "local" train between the two cities. We had booked a bedroom on the *Canadian*, as we would be on the train for three nights. I was, frankly, stunned by how well maintained the cars were, even though they were almost 50 years old. I wish *I* had been in that good shape when I was 50. Our car attendant was a cheerful young woman, who somehow managed to stay cheerful for the entire trip.

The train left Toronto in the evening, and during the night passed out of the metropolitan area and onto the geological feature called the Canadian Shield. This was the most surprising part of the trip. The tourist material promoting the train rightly hypes the mountain portions, and barely mentions the long traverse through the Shield.

"Barren" is the word that comes to mind to describe the scenery. It is low, rocky, and features stunted trees and vegetation. Surprisingly, it was one of the most challenging parts of the route to build, because the rock is so hard

206

it is difficult to blast, and for the workers, the summer insect populations (blackflies, gnats, mosquitoes) made life a maddening hell. The geology is complex, and represents an ancient volcano caldera, a meteor strike, or both.

A "proper" transcontinental train has three locomotives in front.

As you approach within 20 miles or so of the city of Sudbury, you notice a change in the landscape. The vegetation becomes dead and black, with scattered dwarf trees. Then you see the cause of this moonscape. The Inco Corporation *Superstack,* the second tallest smokestack in the world. Turns out that the area around Sudbury is one of the richest regions of Canada for mineral wealth. Iron, nickel, tin, copper, platinum; all the good stuff with which we make our civilization. The mines that extract the ore were established not long after the CP passed through the area, and the processing plants (and their air pollution) soon followed. One response to increasing clamor about smelter emissions was the construction of the 1,250 foot tall *Superstack* in 1970. Six workers were on top of the stack when the Sudbury tornado of 20 August 1970 hit it. All six quit the next day. For railfans, the area around Sudbury has a lot of train activity, much of which can be seen from the *Canadian.*

After leaving the Shield, the terrain was mostly flat or slightly rolling, agricultural, and seemingly devoid of interest until we hit the western foothills. People have often asked me if I don't get bored on one of these long trips. They are often surprised when I say, "Never." There are a variety of reasons for this.

First, you are not confined to a single place, as you are in an airplane, whose coach seats give an excellent simulation of the electric chair, right down to the straps. The *Canadian* during the summer is almost a quarter mile long, so one can take a rather impressive stroll. Next, the seats are infinitely more comfortable than aircoach seats, which give you the opportunity to recreate the sensation of being in the womb. Third, the scenery, although sometimes featureless, as it is in the prairie, is something that nowadays you simply can't see in a car, because there are many stretches of a transcontinental railroad that are dozens of miles from a highway, and you can see the way the country looked before rest stops, McFood restaurants, and Shell stations.

Perhaps the height of the experience is mealtimes. Even on Amtrak, the long distance trains have real restaurant cars (note added, alas, in 2018. On the *Lake Shore Limited,* first-class passengers now get a bag of food, which they take to an attendant, who nukes it), and much of the food is actually cooked on the train, instead of being vaporized by a flight attendant, should you be lucky enough to actually HAVE food on board. There's another wonderful aspect of dining on a train (old saying; animals feed, men eat, gentlemen dine). The dining car tables are usually what is known in the restaurant business as a "four-top," i.e. there are four place settings. That means that if you are a couple, guaranteed you will have another two people sitting with you. Here's where the gods of chance play a role. Sometimes you will sit next to someone absolutely fascinating–or not. On the *Canadian*, there is a higher proportion of interesting people than on most trains, because this one is a travel destination for travelers from all over the world.

If you remember either Hitchcock's "North by Northwest," or the Gene Wilder/Richard Pryor film "Silver Streak," you will recall that this chance meeting of strangers offers at least the theoretical possibility of romance. I can personally attest that this possibility is more than theoretical.

When I was returning to San Francisco from RPI in 1959, via the Santa Fe, I met a girl on board. I recall that she got on in Kansas, and got off at San Bernardino, where she lived with her grandmother. I believe her name was Lynnette. We exchanged addresses, and started a correspondence. After a couple of months, it appeared that it was time for a road trip to San Bernardino.

I had recently acquired a driver's license, and my father had a bright red '55 Chrysler Windsor hardtop, with the automatic transmission lever on the dashboard. I promised him that if he would let me borrow it, I would drive carefully and prudently, and would leave early on a Saturday and return on Sunday. This was a round trip of almost 900 miles, and there were no through freeways. There also wasn't much traffic, and I discovered that the roads through the desert as you approached San Bernardino bore an amazing resemblance to the Bonneville salt flats. So, strictly in the interest of science, I felt obliged to discover what the top speed of a Chrysler Windsor with the 301 cubic inch Spitfire V8 was. 115 miles per hour. Not great, but satisfying. My dad was always mystified why he had to replace his back tires twice as often as his front tires, once he started letting me use his car.

Alas, when I reached San Berdoo, I discovered that both Lynnette and her grandmother were heavily into Jesus, something that had escaped my notice before, so I chalked the visit up to driving practice.

Back to the dining car. We had a number of Canadians as dinner companions, and having the luxury of all the time in the world to talk about everything under the sun, we gained an impression that many Canadians look at the world a bit differently than many Americans. Less interested in rugged individualism, more aware of the social contract. In their views of the proper role of government in affairs, we found many of our traveling companions had views that were rather startlingly different from mainstream American views. That came as a surprise.

Catching the view on *The Canadian*

The feature on the *Canadian* that made boredom almost impossible was the variety of vistas available for quiet sightseeing. You could sit in your bedroom, in total privacy, and watch the muskeg slide by. You could sit in one of the dome cars, with glass ceilings. Best of all was to sit in the last car of the train, the observation car, whose windows wrapped around the rear of the train, giving you a panoramic view of where you just had been

One of the best parts of the *Canadian*'s current route is normally traversed at night; the run through the Fraser and Thompson River canyons from

Kamloops into Vancouver in British Columbia. On this trip, the train was about 6 hours late, so we got to see the astounding feats of civil engineering that were required to push a rail line from the mountains to the coastal plain. Both the CP and CN share this canyon route, shifting back and forth from one side of the river to the other.

Vancouver, BC, the end point of the trip, is a great tourist city dripping with money from trade, tourism, and forestry. There is a strong Chinese influence in the city, largely due to immigration from Hong Kong. Best Dim Sum east of Kowloon. We stayed for about three days, then it was off to Seattle.

Amtrak operated the international service between Vancouver and Seattle using a set of equipment unique to the Portland-Seattle run. The cars were leased Talgo-style tilting models, incongruously pulled by a conventional Amtrak F59 diesel engine. The first car was a "transition car" with a fairing that visually tried to blend the tall engine with the low cars. The effect was not terribly successful, and the result looked more or less like a tadpole, or a sperm. The cars were very comfortable, however, and you couldn't see how funky the train looked from the inside.

When I was a post-doc in Seattle from '67-'69, the town was booming with the arrival of the Boeing 747. Although not directly caused by my departure, Seattle's economy crashed not long after I left, largely due to problems with Boeing. However, the Microsoft revolution starting in the mid-'80s largely brought the city back, and the town was jumpin' during our visit. Seattle had changed tremendously, and I was reminded of Thomas Wolfe's maxim, "You can't go home again." Time and again, as I have revisited the places of my youth, I've found that they've changed so much that I no longer could remember why I liked them. San Francisco and Seattle are still great places to grow up in, but they're not the places *I* grew up in, and there's a certain sadness in that.

We took the Amtrak version of the *Empire Builder* to Chicago, with a several day stop at the Glacier Park Lodge near Glacier Park, Montana. The Glacier Park Lodge is one of a handful of surviving national park hotels like the Ahwanee (now "Majestic Yosemite-" a name that tells you there was some legal business in the renaming) Hotel in Yosemite, or the Crater Lake Lodge in Oregon that can actually, if only for a few days, bring you back to a day when there was no internet, people had more words than "awesome" to describe something very good and "it sucks" to describe something loathsome, despicable, or execrable.

"Red Jammers" at Glacier.

From the lodge, there are a variety of day trips available on a fleet of unique "red jammer" buses built in the 1930s and restored in the early '00s by Ford Motor Company with propane-fueled engines. Built to travel the Going-to-the-Sun Road across Logan Pass, these buses provide the terrified tourist the closest we have in America to the experience of traveling the infamous Troll's Ladder road in Norway. We picked the run to the Prince of Wales hotel just across the Canadian border at Waterton Lake. The Prince of Wales is probably the most stunning place in the world to have High Tea in the afternoon.

Prince of Wales Hotel, Alberta, Canada

After Glacier Park, the rest of the trip to Chicago was a bit of an anticlimax; been there, done that. In the Windy City, we transferred to an Amtrak train that was new to me over most of its route, the *Cardinal*, which goes from Chicago to Washington via Cincinnati, the Shenandoah Valley, and the New River Gorge. At the time of our riding, it also traveled over some of the worst track on the Amtrak system. I've rarely been scared on a train, but trying to get to sleep in the sleeping car as it bounced through Indiana and Ohio, was, frankly, a bit terrifying. I'm POSITIVE we were in no danger (well, almost positive), but it sure as hell felt like the damn car was going to tip over on its side and grind us all into catfood. The current on-time record of the *Cardinal* is execrable (see two paragraphs ago), as it was then. The reason seems to be that the run is one of Amtrak's routes most traveled by really heavy freight trains, which beat hell out of track on curvy stretches. At the time we took the train, track maintenance on the former Conrail route was being reduced to lower expenses to make the company more attractive for future takeover bids.

Alas, in addition to providing us a bone-shaking ride, the poor old *Capitol* got us into Washington just in time to miss the last northbound train to Boston (sleeping car space on the overnight train, the *Night Owl* was sold out at any rate), so we made ourselves comfortable on the benches in Union Station until the first morning train, which left at some ungodly time like 3 am. Today, the descendent of the *Night Owl* doesn't even have a sleeping car. Finally, about 10 am, we got off in Kingston, three weeks and about 7,000 miles after we started. Truly, one of the world's greatest loop train rides, and you can pretty much repeat it today.

Chapter 15

Short Runs

The long, exotic trips are wonderful, but they are usually for special occasions. In between, how is one to satisfy a train Jones, if one is neither rich nor a business traveler? There exist a number of alternatives, although which are practical depends greatly on what part of the country you live in.

Perhaps the most exotic of these alternatives takes advantage of the fact that in the United States, there are still several hundred railroad passenger cars owned by individuals. In condition they range from cars that look like they had been preserved in a time warp since the 1950s, to obscenely luxurious remodeled vehicles that make Donald Trump's Boeing 757 look like a Mumbai taxi. Most of the owners of these cars belong to the American Association of Private Railroad Car Owners, which has to be one of the more exclusive clubs in the world.

Every year, the owners of these cars assemble at some starting point around the US or Canada, and begin a week long joint trip on some spectacular railroad line. The individual cars are attached to the rear of regular Amtrak trains to get to the jumping off point. These trips are called "positioning moves," and the owners of the cars will sometimes sell tickets to "civilians" to ride on all or part of these moves–although most owners are, well, rich, some live in the real world, and are happy to get a little revenue to help with the cost of maintenance.

In the early '90s, I somehow heard about one of these positioning moves for the private car *Caritas,* which had been built in the '40s for the *Texas Special* of the St. Louis-San Francisco Railroad. It was of a type called an open-platform observation car. This meant that there was a little outside

The *only* way to travel.

"porch" with a railing at the end of the car, upon which one could stand and view the passing scene while in communion with the elements. The interior of the car was fitted out with bedrooms, bathrooms, a kitchen, a dining room, and a lounge. Tickets were available for the leg of the trip from Providence to New York Penn Station. As I remember, the ticket was expensive but not obscenely so, and after all, how often do college professors get to travel like millionaires?

The *Caritas* was by no means the most *luxe* of the then-operating private cars, but it sure beat an Amcoach. It was a morning departure, and there was a little breakfast buffet set up in the lounge area. The croissants could be washed down with a mimosa or two. There were about 10 other passengers, and a steward. The owner was going to meet the car in New York, so it was just us railroad buffs. I have to admit that there was a relatively high fraction of foamers in the group, and I quickly exhausted my conversational knowledge of Maine Central boxcar axles.

View from back platform of *Caritas*.

The thing that set this experience quite apart from any other kind of contemporary rail journey was the opportunity to stand out on the back platform. The view to the rear is one that cannot be enjoyed on regular Amtrak trains today, and add to it the experience of standing on the back platform as the train swooshed around the curves on the Connecticut coastline; oh my! Things began to change from pleasant to spectacular once we passed through New Haven. The right-of-way widened to four tracks, and the massive infrastructure needed to provide electricity to the electric locomotives had a Victorian feeling to it, given that it had been originally installed in 1907. The neighborhoods the line passed through after leaving New Rochelle were gritty and garbage strewn, and one had the impression that both sides of the track were on the wrong side. We would occasionally pass a commuter train, and of course, I was compelled to wave at the engineer.

I had tried to mentally prepare myself for what the view would be like as

Approach to the Hell Gate Bridge.

we climbed the approach viaduct and then passed through the Hell Gate
Bridge, but my efforts were for naught; it was stunning. On the left (facing
backwards) was the skyline of New York, set off by the saved-in-the-nick-
of-time Citigroup Center building, and on the right were the Throgs Neck
and Whitestone Bridges. The track sails over Astoria, Queens, on a high
viaduct, past the childhood homes of Tony Bennett and Ethyl Merman
(and the burial place of Mafia "Prime Minister" Frank Costello). The
viaduct then gradually slopes down, and bears west to ground level, past the
old Harold interlocking tower and the Sunnyside passenger car yard. Then,
without much warning, the track dips down below ground level, and
plunges into the east portal of one of the East River railroad tunnels.

From the back platform of *Caritas*, the ride through the tunnel was both
exhilarating and terrifying. The noise level was stupefying, and the
darkness was penetrated only by light from the "refuges;" little alcoves

218

built into the walls for any worker unfortunate enough to be on the tracks when a train comes through. When your eyes adapted, you saw that this tunnel was not like an ordinary railroad tunnel. The tracks are actually at the bottom of a concrete trench, only a little wider than the car itself, and coming up to a level just below the car windows. The idea apparently is that if a train derails in the tunnel, instead of being able to penetrate the wall of the tube, allowing the East River to flow into the basement of Penn Station, the derailed train would remain confined to the trench. The effect was remarkably like being in a real-time version of the famed Trench Run on the Death Star in *Star Wars*, except you were going backwards, and there weren't any XX-9 heavy turbolaser towers. I can't be sure exactly how fast we were going, but it certainly exceeded my speed comfort level. The train began to slow, and we exited the tunnel onto the maze of trackwork leading into Penn Station. The visual impression was much like that of the subway scenes in "The Taking of Pelham One Two Three." I did see a couple of the famous rats scurrying about, and immediately put Underground Track Inspector much higher on my list of Jobs I Don't Want. Ever.

All of *Caritas'* passengers got off at Penn, and dispersed on their various errands. I dropped over to the venerable Olden Camera on Broadway that used to be one of the best places in New York if you liked antique cameras and spirited haggling. After wandering about for a couple of hours, I headed back to Penn Station, and caught the next Amtrak regional back home. Everything is relative, and "Business Class" on the regional isn't really bad, but in contrast to *Caritas*, I was reminded of the slogan of the now defunct men's cologne for men called *Pullman*; "There's No Class Like First Class."

During much of the last 40 years, I've spent a lot of time with a local historic preservation organization in Rhode Island called The Friends of the Kingston Station. The group got the station completely restored in the '90s, and remains active. Most of the members are historic preservationists, rather than railfans or foamers, but over the years, we've had some Amtrak employees be active participants. The group also works officially with Amtrak and the Rhode Island Department of Transportation, which owns the building. As a consequence of contacts made through the organization (and perhaps the result of thousands of hours of volunteer work), I've had some train opportunities that most railfans would kill for.

Several of our members have been engineers, and once I hitched a ride in the cab of an AEM-7 electric engine from Kingston to Boston with an Amtrak engineer friend from the group named Chris Perrone. Chris was one of the last Amtrak engineers qualified to operate electric, diesel, AND steam locomotives. On weekends, he operated some of the steam locomotives of the Valley Railroad in Connecticut as a volunteer. It was after dark when I got on board. I had ridden in engine cabs before, and I somehow expected the noise level in an electric locomotive to be lower than a diesel, but it was just as loud, but of a different nature; more compressors hissing, and relays clacking. The AEM-7's ("meatballs") had a flat front, so the view forward was unobstructed (and a bit scarey, the first time).

The basic controls of either a diesel or electric locomotive are pretty simple, but I knew the training period for engineers was quite long, and you had to be "qualified" for a specific piece of the route. I asked Chris what the difference was between a highly skilled engineer and a so-so one. He explained that one of the marks of professional pride that engineers used to more-or-less show off to other engineers was accuracy and economy of movement in stopping. Say what?

Trains use air brakes, and these are not applied by foot, as in a car, but with a handle on the "dashboard." Once the handle is in a particular position, it applies a certain amount of pressure on the brake discs until the train stops. This pressure is constant, as if you pressed down on the brake pedal in a car with a constant amount of foot pressure, and didn't vary it until the car came to a halt. In reality, in a car you continuously vary your foot pressure as you sense that you're going to stop either short of, or beyond the place you wanted to end up. You can do the same thing in a train, constantly adjusting the position of the brake lever as you determine the rate at which the train slows so that it finally stops at the point you wanted, say at a station platform. But this back-and-forth might change the rate of deceleration, jostling the passengers waiting in the aisle in preparation for getting off. The virtuoso way to stop a train, however, was to somehow detect how much the train weighed (which would help determine how much brake pressure it would take to stop it), then make a single, gentle brake adjustment some distance away from the point where you wanted to stop. You would then not touch the brake handle until the train came to a halt. The passengers would only be aware of a slow, steady deceleration.

I sort of understood this, then Chris said he would show me how it worked for the Boston Route 128 station stop. Some miles away from the station, for no apparent reason, he made a gentle brake application. He explained that he could tell how much the train weighed (which would vary with the number of passengers) by how fast the train slowed with a given brake application. Armed with this knowledge, he told me that he was going to stop at Route 128 with the nose of the engine just shy of the front end of the station platform, with a single application of the brakes. He had slowed the train down to about 40 mph after leaving Canton Junction, and about a mile before the Route 128 station, he slid the brake lever over, almost "feeling" it as it went. He then took his hand off the lever and folded his arms. We almost imperceptibly slowed, and gently slid into the station. When the train stopped, the nose of the engine was about 4 feet shy of the front end of the platform. I was in awe. I gave Chris a *Wayne's World* "We are not worthy" bow, he chuckled, and we pulled out of the station. This was like Babe Ruth's called shot in the 1932 World Series.

The remaining short run into Boston from Route 128 station had an almost science-fiction quality to it. After leaving Route 128 station, the track passes by the MBTA yard at Readville, and a train can maintain a good clip until the junction with the MBTA Orange Line at Forest Hills station. Then it starts to get interesting. The tracks begin to drop below grade, until they are essentially operating in a walled trench. The Amtrak inbound track is next to one of these walls, and a train traveling about 60 FEELS like it is going more than a hundred. At night, you can see the street lights far above your head, but the track is illuminated only by the engine's headlights. For you old timers, the visual effect has a startling similarity to the slit-scan "Star-Gate" sequence from Stanley Kubrick's *2001*. Closest *I'll* ever come to traveling at warp speed. At the Mass Avenue MBTA station, the tracks dive underground, and the sensation brought back childhood memories of the old Giant Dipper roller coaster at Santa Cruz, California, which immediately drops into what seems to be a bottomless pit-tunnel after leaving the station. I suppose if you do it every day, you get used to it, but I was shaking when the train stopped at Back Bay, I thanked Chris, and got

In the cab of an AEM-7 going 115 mph.

off with a whole new respect for railroad engineers.

The other to-die-for cab ride I experienced came through the same association with the Friends of the Kingston Station. At the time, Amtrak was offering "inspection rides" to members of groups they thought might be useful to them. As the Friends had negotiated 10 years of rent-free use of Kingston Station for them, we fit in this category. The deal was, three of us in the lucky group got to ride in the rear cab of the Acela from Providence to Penn Station, under the "supervision" of the conductor of the train. On the Acela trains, the rear cab is "cut out" during operation, so an accidental jostling of the controls by a klutzy visitor would have no effect.

The author at controls of Acela. Note from the position of his hands he is not actually CONTROLLING the Acela.

The surprising first impression of the cab when swinging aboard was how confining it seemed. Compared to a "Meatball" conventional electric engine, the windows were tiny, and the first thought I had was that the interior was more like the inside of a tank than a locomotive. This claustrophobic feeling was, I suppose, not entirely irrational. The cabs of American locomotives are much stronger than their European counterparts because, unfortunately, American trains are much more likely to hit vehicles at road crossings than are European trains.

Compared to an airliner cockpit, the dashboard was uncluttered, and actually rather elegant, in soft shades of gray and blue. The three main operating controls were throttle, brake, and reverse levers. There were two engineer's seats, although usually, a one-person crew was at the controls (query to self; can one person be a "crew"?). Once we got rolling, I was once again caught off guard by how rough riding an electric engine is, even the Acela's power unit. It was also quite noisy, unlike the very quiet Acela cars. When we got to the first stretch of 150 mph track in Rhode Island, about 25 miles southwest of Providence, we had our first hint that although the Acela was a slowpoke compared to its European or Asian contemporaries, you very definitely had a sensation of speed. Looking backwards from a fast moving-a VERY fast moving-train is unsettling, especially when you pull into a station and stop. You have the uncanny sensation that the landscape is still moving, but in the reverse direction. This is the closest non-drug demonstration you can have to the fact that your eyes can sometimes deceive you.

From New Haven to New Rochelle, we were on Metro North tracks, but then at New Rochelle the four track main line continued west as the old New Haven Harlem River line, and we switched over to Amtrak owned tracks that eventually led to the Hell Gate bridge. This short stretch of line was haunted by the ghosts of railroads past. The right of way was clearly wide enough for at least four, and in some places 6 tracks. Until 1937, the tracks of the New York, Westchester, and Boston commuter railroad paralleled what eventually became the Amtrak route to Penn Station. These tracks were removed during WWII. This was almost certainly an unwise move in retrospect, because this stretch of double track now provides a

Harlem River Line. Note deteriorated condition of right of way.

severe bottleneck for Northeast Corridor trains from New York to Boston.

As it was on the *Caritas,* the climb up the viaduct to the Hell Gate Bridge was breathtaking, but this time, I was concentrating on the route and the bridge, rather than the surrounding scenery. The span was completed in 1916, and at the time was the longest steel arch bridge in the world. From a distance, the structure appears massive, but going through it, the hangers (vertical beams) seem surprisingly delicate. Today, two of the three tracks are for passenger trains, and are electrified

Hell Gate Bridge from back cab of Acela.

After the mind-numbing trip through the East River tunnel, we pulled into Penn Station "on the advertised" (railroad slang for on time). Our conductor-host took us through some of the crew-only passageways to his destination, the crew ready room, and we parted company there. After the inevitable wandering around through the rabbit warren of underground passageways, we found our way to what passes for a waiting room in the disgraceful contemporary Penn Station. The trip back in coach on a Regional train reached a new high for anticlimax.

There are many other possibilities for short, interesting trips for rail enthusiasts that don't require *knowing a guy*, (a favorite Rhode Island expression). There are several national railroad history organizations that have local or regional chapters that own passenger cars in operating condition. Every once in a while, they'll hook one up behind an Amtrak train, and sell tickets to the public. They also have national conventions in locations of railroad interest. There's usually a "fan trip" associated with these meetings. For example, the Railway and Locomotive Historical

226

Society met in 2014 in Ely, Nevada, location of the Nevada Northern Railroad. The other big national organization, the National Railway Historical Society, has dozens of local chapters. An online search would be the easiest way to track these organizations down.

In most parts of the United States, there are relatively accessible (and affordable) "tourist railroads" that can give you at least a taste of what train riding was in the glory days. New England is fortunate in having a population density high enough to support a number of these little lines, most of which are run, or assisted by volunteers. True, you will not be able to recreate the experience of walking down the red carpet toward your drawing room on the *Twentieth Century Limited*, but many of the tourist lines have a lovingly cared for old teapot locomotive, and for kids whose closest acquaintance to a steam locomotive is Thomas, they won't notice that 'ol 93 is really a freight locomotive that came from the East Grunion and Hadleyville Railroad rather than the line it runs on now. Many of the dozens of railroad museums around the country also offer short rides. Unfortunately, the necessity to be attractive to families with small children, these museums' largest clientele, means that it is difficult to have a "pure" ride that recreates the experience of being on a train a half century ago. One must put up with fake train robberies, folk singers wandering up the isles singing "Casey Jones," conductors carrying digital pocket watches, and engineers wearing striped bib overalls and caps, something that hasn't been seen on a "real" railroad for decades. I tend to be phlegmatic about such things. Without all the corny stuff, these tiny lines probably wouldn't survive, and their wonderful old equipment would be sent to China to be melted down and made into door knobs

227

Chapter 16

End of the Line

When I was a graduate student at UC Davis in the mid-'60s, I used to "commute" between Davis and San Francisco, about an 80 mile run. By this time, my train options were few, so I usually took the *Shasta Daylight*, which by then was a pale shadow of its former self.

For some reason, I usually rode in the first coach, and there was usually the same "chair car porter," as attendants were called then. He was an old guy who looked sort of like Satchel Paige. He'd been with the railroad for thirty years plus.

Passengers destined for San Francisco got off the train at Oakland 16th Street Station to catch their bus for The City, ferry service having been discontinued in 1957. As the train slowed at Emeryville, this porter always walked up the aisle to the head of the car, turned around, and addressed the tired passengers:

"Folks, we comin' in to Oakland. This here train don't go no further, unless you wanta' swim. You goin' to San Francisco, you got to get off this train here. This is the last stop, and this train ain't goin' nowhere til' it goes back to Portland, so if you wants to go to San Francisco, you got to get off and take the bus. This is the end of the line, folks, soooo—."

"Good bye, Oakland, hellooOOOO San Francisco!"

Then he did a fast little buck-and-wing, and everybody got off.

So then, this too is the end of the line for this very long journey. There have been quite a few train rides in Europe in the last few years, including Prague-Vienna, Florence-Rome, and Amsterdam-Paris, but only one that ranks as a world-class rail enthusiast trip; the Flåm line in Norway.

This short (13 miles) branch line climbs 2,800 feet from its origin in Flåm, a small port on the Sognefjord, to Myrdal, a station on the Bergen-Oslo main line. This produces a grade of 5.8%, the steepest mainline in the world. It also means that the passenger trains that run on it have only 6 cars and require two handsome 7,200 HP electric locomotives.

The line's beauty is also its curse. It *crawls* with tourists. This seems to be the downside of increasing population and prosperity. I used to like hiking around Mt. Washington in New Hampshire. Today 50 million people live within a six hour drive, and a large fraction of them like to hike (and/or browse the outlet shops near the mountain).

"Surely, we can fit a few more in."

The Flåm trip was not planned as such. Neither Marjorie nor I had ever been to Norway nor heard of the Flåm, and although all of our previous travels (with the exception of a cruise or two) had been "independent," we decided to try a guided bus tour for a change. We had a certain amount of trepidation. What if you get stuck with a VAP (Very Annoying Person) in the confined quarters of your bus? The question did not go unanswered. We had both an irritating foursome and an obnoxious couple sharing our quarters, but they were easy to avoid.

However, we made a discovery. Unless one of your annoyers is Freddy Krueger, after a couple of days, you can just tune them out. The tour guide does not have that luxury, however, and other than armpit sniffer (yes, it actually exists), I cannot imagine a tougher job.

Half the trip was by tour bus, a quarter by boat, and a quarter by train–not just the Flåm run, but a mainline mountain stretch from Myrdal to Bergen. Not long after leaving Myrdal, the train passes through the 6-mile long Finse tunnel. Not much of a view inside the tunnel, but the mountain vistas on either end are stunning.

Flåm engine at Myrdal.

There was one other out-of-the-ordinary trip that deserves mention, mostly because it was to such an odd (to most Americans) place. In the mid-'90s, when I was still working as an ornithologist, I got an inquiry from a young man who was a graduate student in Slovenia (no, not Slovakia, which is quite different) who politely inquired if I would be on his doctoral thesis committee. I am embarrassed to admit I had to look up where Slovenia was. It is the northernmost remnant of the old Yugoslavia, and is to the east of Venice, the south of Austria, the north of Croatia, and the west of Hungary. It is about six times the size of Rhode Island. The Slovene language appears to be allergic to vowels, to wit, the capitol city is Ljubljana.

The young man's name was Iztok, and as it turned out, he had a brilliant dissertation. I did my usual thesis committee stuff by correspondence, then out of the blue, I got a letter from his department asking me if I would do them the honour (sic) of serving as chairman of his oral doctoral thesis defense in Slovenia. Naturally, they would be delighted to pay all my expenses, and throw in a couple of extra days' stay to compensate me for my troubles. Now, this was at a time when both the Slovenian and US economies were smokin' hot.

Alas, they couldn't quite see their way to making it a Business Class trip, and I had to make two tight plane changes, the last of which involved a sprint between terminals which revealed to me that I was much too old for this kind of crap any longer.

The approach to the Ljubljana airport from Munich runs over the little-known (outside the area), but spectacular Julian Alps. Iztok and his wife Maja, who is a high school English teacher met me at the airport. They got me established at my hotel, and for several hours I wandered around the delightful, and relatively undiscovered city.

Next day, Iztok passed his exam with flying colors, and he and Maja said that they would be my tour guides for the next few days, and what did I want to see? Somehow, accidently I suppose, the fact that I was a railfan dropped into the conversation. Surprisingly, they didn't think that this was at all unusual or weird–Slovenia was a major rail crossroads in Europe, the railroad was a large employer, and there were enough railfans to support a weekly two-hour long steam train ride through the mountains. The national railroad museum was in Ljubljana, but unfortunately, it was closed on the only day I had available.

However, I discovered that Slovenia, like Rhode Island, followed the "I know a guy" principle. Iztok must have had a friend of a friend, because arrangements were made to open the museum for me. I am embarrassed to say that it would put many US railroad museums to shame, especially given that the whole country only had twice the population of Rhode Island. One unusual feature of the railroad museum was a large exhibit on the evolution

Signals display room, National Railway Museum of Slovenia.

National Railway Museum of Slovenia. The author is checking for ghosts on the tracks.

of signaling technology--semaphores, searchlight signals, etc.,

I had also mentioned that I liked wine, and grew my own wine grapes, so they arranged a day trip that would let us combine trains and wine. From Ljubljana, there is a road heading toward the Adriatic Sea that passes through Slovenia's wine district, and winds its way through the coastal karst, or limestone foothills. Karst areas are where the world's great caves are found, and Slovenia has a beauty-the Postojna cave.

The cave was opened to the public in the early 19th century, and in 1874, tracks were laid in the cave for a train to enable visitors to more easily visit the interior. Over the years, this railroad has been expanded and improved, and today, there is a two-track narrow gauge railroad that has a loop at both ends. The round trip run is four miles, and the trains are electric powered, and resemble amusement park trains. It is, to my knowledge, the only cave train in the world (other than, of course, the tacky old-fashioned Cave Train dark ride at the Santa Cruz, California boardwalk that doesn't really run in a cave).

The end of the road from Ljubljana was the little coastal town of Koper, which is a port city with extensive rail yards connecting with its docks. Away from the port area, the town itself was charming, and its architecture reminiscent of Venice.

On the way back to Ljubljana, we stopped at a number of train stations where I could get the obligatory train pictures. Slovenian trains did not have luxo service, but they were clean, fast, and attractive. In places, they

Koper, Slovenia.

used the old-fashioned semaphore signaling system. After several more days of sightseeing around Ljubljana and the Alpine foothills, it was time to come back to Little Rhody.

Ljubljana station.

So, after 70 years (more or less) of train riding, how does the train riding experience compare today with, say, 50 years ago? It's sort of like my favorite good news/bad news joke.

This guy walks into a doctor's office for some routine tests. A couple of days later, he gets a call from the doctor, and the doctor says, "Mr. Jones, we just got the results of your tests, and I have some good news, and I have some bad news for you. Which do you want first?"

"Let me have the good news first."

"Well, all the tests said the same thing. You have 24 hours to live."

"24 hours to live! Wait a minute, Doc. You said that was the GOOD news. If that was the good news, what could the bad news possibly be?'

"Well, I tried to call you yesterday, but you didn't pick up--."

From the perspective of the traveler, the arc of change of passenger rail transportation describes a "U" from the '50s to the present, at least in the United States. After WWII, US passenger trains were dismal, but the trains of the early Eisenhower era were wonderful, both for coach and sleeping car passengers. The coach seats were much bigger than today's, and the fare was about the same, adjusted for inflation. The dining cars were real restaurants, and the SP had its own house bottled wine. There was more choice of routes and trains.

Then, with the start of the Interstate Highway System in 1956, and the introduction of the Boeing 707 into commercial airline service a few years later, both enterprises heavily subsidized by the federal government (note: the airline industry doesn't like to talk about this much), the passenger train began an extraordinarily rapid decline such that by the start of Amtrak service in 1970, there were only a handful of decent trains left in the United States, all but one of which was based in the West. Within a year of its founding, Amtrak cut the number of trains in the system by half. In a number of cases, the trains were so bad, these were mercy killings.

Within a decade, the dedicated railroad passenger like myself found his image changing from sophisticated global traveler to eccentric afraid-to-fly dweeb. While European and Asian passenger train systems were expanding and upgrading, poor little Amtrak, Congress' favorite whipping boy, appeared to be a passenger on a hell-bound train to oblivion.

But then a funny thing happened. There's an old saying, "It's an ill wind that blows no good." The Great Recession of 2008 was bad for most people, but it turned out to be terrific for Amtrak. Amtrak ridership, which had been slowly increasing since 2000, spiked in 2008-2009. Gas was expensive, air fares were up, unemployment was up, and all of a sudden riding a train didn't seem so eccentric any more. Amtrak management capitalized on this increase, and gained new congressional support. There was talk of buying (did I hear that right?) *new cars and locomotives!* There was serious, or semi-serious talk about new *genuinely* high speed rail lines.

However, the impact of the changed climate for Amtrak on the traveler like Yours Truly has so far been minimal, except the trains tend to be more crowded, and there is less all-pervasive gloom among train crews. However, now for the first time in many years, we can see a glimmer of what remained in Pandora's box after all the misery was let loose–Hope. It is probably too much to expect that rail travel in America will generally return to the level of quality it had in the '50s, but if you are willing to leave the country, there are still some stunning train rides around the world that are actually more or less affordable to surviving middle-class folks like me. There are also quite a few genuine *luxe* journeys available to The Elect, but they'll set you back ten grand or so per couple.

Probably the most spectacular regular rail runs that you can take for a modest price are a few in America, and many in Switzerland, Norway, or Sweden. The American runs would have to include the *California Zephyr, Coast Starlight, Adirondack*, and if you can put up with the delays, the *Empire Builder*. A couple of hundred bucks will still get you a round trip through some of the most breathtaking scenery in the world, if you go only between the scenic points. The catch is that you'll probably have to take EconoAir to get to the starting and ending points. If you want to try the European trains on a modest budget, you have to fly to Europe and if you are more than four feet tall, you have to allow yourself a day after arrival to uncurl from the fetal position you have been clamped in for the endless hours aboard the 787 "Dreamliner." Dreamliner? Well, I suppose they couldn't call it "Nightmareliner," could they?

In Switzerland, probably the best regular runs are the two international routes to Italy through the Simplon and St. Gotthard passes, the Loëtschberg line between Interlaken and Brig, and the *Glacier Express* between Zermatt and St. Moritz. A Eurailpass doesn't let you travel on the latter, but gives you a good discount. The list of jaw-clenching mountain railroads is almost endless, but the must-do's include the Pilatus,

Gornergrat Bahn, Jungfraubahn, Brienz Rothorn Bahn, and Rigi-Bahnen. Most of these charge a relatively expensive fare for the length of the ride, but then it's a short ride (at least horizontally). While you're in Switzerland, allow time to visit the Swiss Museum of Transport in Lucerne. There you can see a preserved example of the stunning and significant "Krokodil" locomotives. Norway has some sensational train rides, including the world-class Oslo-Sognefjord-Flåm-Bergen run. In Sweden, you can go from Stockholm to Narvik, beyond the Arctic Circle.

Despite the almost universal use of air travel by well-situated folks, there are still enough hang-the-expense travelers to support a dozen *ultra-luxe* contemporary trains around the world. Perhaps the most pricey is the *Golden Eagle Trans-Siberian Express/Shangri-La Express* between Beijing and Moscow. The cost is as high as the name is long; about $88,000 a couple (flight to Moscow extra) for the 21 day trip. Unbelievably, most of these trains sell out months in advance. In addition to the *ultra-luxe* trains, there are another two dozen or so regular trains whose first class service comes close to the old days. The closest we approach to anything like that in the United States on Amtrak is first class on the *Acela* trains.

And what of the railfan? Is he/she an endangered, or nearly extinct species? Certainly the number of railfans is down compared to, say, the '60s, but there's a fairly simple reason for that. Most hard-core railfans got started as kids, when they were awed by the big, fast, and powerful trains they saw thundering down the tracks near their houses. Now, with the number of rail lines sharply reduced and the consolidation of rail lines, most kids today never actually SEE a real live train up-close and personal. And "keeping consists" as I did as a grad student, is sort of pointless when all the passenger cars you see belong to Amtrak.

Young railfan.

Nonetheless, trains are *still* big, fast, and powerful, and if a kid lives close to an active rail line, they continue to exercise their magic. I'm curator of a local volunteer railroad museum in Rhode Island, and we have generations of kids who started hanging around the museum as sub-teens, and now that they're in the 20's, despite having (very patient) lovers, they still delight in trains. And the vast majority of them are not geeks or nerds. One of our museum "alumni," as a matter of fact, works for Amtrak and is a very cool young man who drives a BMW.

As I approached the end of this book, I found myself asking over and over, "Why trains? Why would any sane person voluntarily spend over 12,000 hours of his life on a train? What is qualitatively different about a train than any other method of conveyance? Trains are old-fashioned, and neither fast nor reliable (at least in the United States), so why bother?"

I think these are reasonable questions, and I have a few suggested answers. First, trains exist on a human scale. You look at one as you get on board, and you can pretty much figure out how it works. It goes where it's going because it's on tracks. There's a big thing up front with a motor that drives wheels that pull it. It travels (most of the time) at speeds not dramatically different than those you drive on a freeway. Its movements are slow and gentle. There's nothing strange or mysterious about anything a train does. Boring, perhaps, but comforting.

Now, get on a plane. Why doesn't it drop out of the sky? What does "a little turbulence" mean? Why don't the wings snap off when they bend up like that? Didn't I read that the temperature outside is -58° at cruising altitude? I've ridden about as many miles on the airlines as I have on the railroads and I'm a private pilot, but every time we're on the approach to landing on a commercial flight, my pulse rate goes up in a way that hardly ever happens when #2171 pulls into Penn Station. Flying is exciting, to be sure, but hardly comforting or relaxing.

A train ride, especially a long distance one, gives you a commodity that is becoming more precious than rubies these days--time to think. You can make a little cocoon for yourself in a train seat. The sound of the moving train doesn't have to be blocked off with earphones. You can get yourself a cuppa Joe and an AmDanish from the café car, go back to your seat, and you *know* you're going to have hours and hours without even the possibility of your thoughts being interrupted by hearing, "The captain has turned on the seatbelt sign. Please return to your seats." That time can be used for reading, sleeping, or best of all, just looking out the window. During that time, should you decide to take advantage of it, your brain can relax for a brief respite from our all-too-connected days.

A train ride gives you an attachment with the landscape that is virtually impossible to get any other way today. Back in the prop plane days, airliners flew low enough so that you could actually make some geographic sense out of what you saw. You could see roads, bridges, little towns, and how they were situated next to each other. Now, except in the arid west, there is usually some kind of cloud deck between your plane and the ground, and even when there isn't, the small towns become vanishingly small.

You could, of course, drive through the landscape in a car, but if you're

240

the driver and doing your job, you won't see any of the scenery. If you're a passenger, you can view the geography, but one Burger King looks pretty much like another as you go across the country on a freeway. In many cases railroad tracks run through areas where there are no roads, and you can see the very same sights your forebears saw in 1870, exactly as they saw them. For kids, if their devices can be pried from their tiny clutched little hands, it is a marvelous learning experience.

Waiting for someone special.

Finally, trains present you with the possibility of pleasant visual anticipation. At wayside stations like mine, Kingston, Rhode Island, if you are picking someone up you can wait on the platform for their train. You can look up the track and see the rails converge at infinity. You *know* that their train is going to arrive on that track. At an airport, you wait in a congested corridor, presenting you with infinite opportunities to purchase overpriced snacks and airsick pills. You have no idea from what direction the plane you're waiting for is coming from, and you usually can't see it land.

With any kind of luck, about three minutes before the train is scheduled to arrive, you can see a pinprick of light at the joining of the rails on the horizon. If the person you are waiting for is important to you, your heart begins to beat faster, but in a good way. The light gets larger and brighter, and soon you can make out the outline of the engine. The sound of the locomotive begins to reach you; a powerful basso sound, but understandable and comforting, not a screaming outer-spacey whine.

Soon, with a screeching of brakes, the train comes to a halt, and the guessing game can begin. Which car is she on? You scan up and down the train, then you see her, fifth car from the front. She descends the stairs and gives you a wave-your wait is over.

And that's why I love trains.

The End

About the Author

FRANK HEPPNER was born in San Francisco, and for 41 years was a Professor of Biological Sciences at the University of Rhode Island. He was part of one of the teams that developed the first computer simulations of bird flocks in the mid '80s. He built his first model airplane when he was five, and his first scratch-built HO model train boxcar when he was 13. He loves trains, and has ridden over 500,000 miles by rail around the world. For many years he was a volunteer pilot for the Civil Air Patrol. He has written six books and over 60 scientific articles. He has been active in civic affairs in Rhode Island, including the North Kingstown Conservation Commission, the South Kingstown Public Housing Authority, where he served as Chair for many years, and he was the Chairman of the Board of Directors of the Friends of the Kingston Railroad Station, a volunteer group that restored the historic structure.

Made in the
USA
Middletown, DE